Ethel A. Matthews
7/3/72

JUNE PLATT'S

New England

Cook Book

JUNE PLATT'S

New England Cook Book

With an Introduction by
JAMES BEARD

Atheneum • *New York*

THIS BOOK IS DEDICATED TO

Maine

New Hampshire

Vermont

Massachusetts

Rhode Island

Connecticut

Author's Note

Several years ago, having been assigned the delightful task of writing a New England cook book, while feasting with my publisher, Alfred Knopf, Jr., and my friend James Beard at New York's fabulous Four Seasons restaurant, I returned eagerly and joyfully to our little house in Little Compton, Rhode Island, and began consulting my collection of cook books, over 600 of them. Poring over those relating to New England food, rereading my own books and articles, and recalling memorable New England meals, I was soon knee-deep in recipes to be enjoyed. As I have in recent years devoted a good deal of time and attention to French food, it was a change of pace to concentrate instead on Slumps and Toots and Dowdys, to say nothing of Grunts and Buckles and Fannie Daddies. But it has been more than rewarding, and I can in good conscience recommend that you, too, desert your Larousse and Brillat-Savarin for a while.

I found in the August 1936 issue of *House and Garden* an article I had written for Dick Wright, in which I had quoted from the foreword by Frank Crowninshield to the English translation of Brillat-Savarin's *Physiology of Taste*, as follows: "Where lies the body of that mute American who first married the pork to the bean? And name if you can the early citizen of Boston who suspected that between Cod-Fish and Brown Bread raged a mysterious, almost illicit Amour."

From *The Regional Cook Book* by Ruth Berolzumer, published in 1939 by Culinary Arts Institute (book 24 of my collection) I learned that New England's chowders and boiled dinners originated when the Pilgrims from the British Isles were faced with what to do with codfish, clams, mussels, corn from the Indians, and game from the forests. Later they themselves planted corn, pumpkins, beans, turnips, onions, peas, and carrots. The fruits available were wild strawberries, huckleberries, gooseberries, grapes, plums, and raspberries. Then they discovered eels (oh dear) and, thank goodness, lobsters. It seems that oats and corn were the grains most used. The cattle brought from England multiplied, and then New Englanders had milk and butter. The maple trees in Vermont produced maple syrup —characterized by the use of maple sugar in Vermont. The fresh-water fish available were brook trout, shad, and pickerel. Walnuts, hickory nuts, butternuts, and chestnuts were also at hand. (Alas, try to find hickory nuts in this day and age.)

In 1934, having sold our farm in New Jersey, and soon thereafter having acquired a pretty piece of property in Little Compton, Rhode Island, my husband Joe and I proceeded to build our beloved first house, nestled down into what remained of the foundation of an old barn blown away in a cruel hurricane. We called it Cherry Cottage—because we had hopefully planted on either side of the front door two espalier cherry trees, which promptly died. One of our early joys, particularly on weekends, was taking the night boat from New York to Providence, with

car aboard, plus two lively sons, John and Peter, headed for
Little Compton. On the very first trip, cold and tired, we were
comforted aboard with a truly hot and steaming New England
clam chowder, rich and creamy with potatoes and milk (no
tomatoes).

On another trip, having reached the Lobster Pot in Bristol,
starved as always, we encountered New England Black Chowder and Grapenut Pudding. What made the chowder black I
never found out, but know only that it was. The Lobster Pot
just wouldn't part with their recipe. As for the Grapenut Pudding, we soon discovered that it was included on any self-
respecting menu in New England. It is to this day a family
favorite of ours.

On many future trips, another joy was eating in our garden
surrounded by Brownell roses and Friend lilacs. Nine times out
of ten, we reveled in something or other cooked over charcoal
in two large terra-cotta buckets acquired down south, where
they are used for heating—not eating.

With three colorful metal tables and twelve chairs securely
anchored on the pebbled space between the garden and kitchen,
we could and did gather around us as many as ten of our Little
Compton friends or weekend guests from New York or there-
abouts. I could, but won't recall all the feasts we had, but two
memorable ones are worth particular mention: one for Juliana
Force of the Whitney Museum, and another for Richardson
Wright of *House and Garden,* who had come all the way from
New York to entertain our garden club with a lecture on "The
Migration of Flowers from One Spot to Another, Thanks to
Birds."

For the Juliana Force party, Joe decided we would have grilled
lobsters as the *pièce de résistance.* Ten lobsters were purchased
at the Liberton Fish Market early in the morning, destined

to be split alive by heartless Joe and willing assistants on our return from the beach.

Waving gaily goodbye to our dear and wonderful Portuguese helper Louise as we left for the beach, I instructed her to please keep the lobsters cool and comfortable during our absence—now in a great big galvanized washtub near the garage —by spraying them with cold water from the water hose. Louise gave me a fleeting, questioning look, but obeyed my orders. On my return from the beach, ahead of our guests, I was greeted by Louise in tears, with the disastrous news that the lobsters, one and all, were dead. I had learned, to my horror, that lobsters don't do well—in fact, die promptly—unless kept on ice or in running salt water. Louise, having been born in New England, knew of course that, being from New York, I was sadly misinformed on the care of lobsters.

This calamity was saved by Brillat-Savarin's Tunafish Omelette, thanks to the fact that I had on hand a supply of canned tunafish and two dozen wonderfully fresh big brown eggs, supplied by Rhode Island Reds—and, believe it or not, the essential Parmesan cheese, and a big supply of garden lettuce, with chives for the omelette and fresh tarragon for the salad, from my own garden.

No one seemed unhappy at the change of menu, having been consoled with Joe's expertly prepared drinks before lunch, and plenty of white wine with the omelette. Louise's heavenly Portuguese bread also did its share toward turning a disaster into a feast.

To continue with the party for the Little Compton Garden Club members and Dick Wright—we all almost fainted from the heat, as our midsummer meeting and lecture had to be held in the upstairs studio, the only place we could provide space enough. But food was served in the garden, where everyone promptly recovered and ate and drank up everything in sight. The grand finale was, for dessert, a cool and refreshing gigantic half of a watermelon filled with orange sherbet and all the fresh fruit and berries in season, drenched with champagne and Curaçao, and topped at the last moment with a shower of confectioner's sugar and blanched almonds. (See page 145 for the recipe.) Ladyfingers, if I remember correctly, were also provided.

In the beginning, my intention was to keep the recipes in this book strictly Early New England, but bit by bit I found myself including present-day treats encountered everywhere in New England, especially with our Little Compton gourmet friends.

As I write this in my Whitehall apartment in Haverford, Pennsylvania, I see before me a handsome (alas, cracked) gigantic crystal pitcher which has come down through our family, and which Daniel Webster and Henry Clay were served beer while debating with each other in Boston on political subjects. I might digress at this point to say that our pitcher is now filled with a once ravishing bouquet of artificial pink, red, and cream-colored tissue-paper roses acquired in Mexico some years ago. And so life goes on.

And now, thirty-five years after the publication of my first cook book, *The June Platt Party Cook Book,* I present you with what may be my last cook book, though I'm not promising that at all.

JUNE PLATT

Introduction

June Platt occupies a place of honor in American cookery, in the company of the great ladies of the nineteenth and early twentieth centuries who paved the way in culinary taste. She has long given us imaginative writing about food, with sly, charming asides about recipes and people. And her recipes have a remarkable stamp of individuality, unlike that of any other food writer. She is undoubtedly one of the most important gastronomic authorities this country has produced.

Mrs. Platt was claimed as a discovery by the late Richardson Wright, the effervescent and discriminating editorial genius who really created *House & Garden*. She wrote for that magazine over a period of years, and many of her contributions were incorporated into her *Plain and Fancy Cook Book*, *Party Cook Book* and *The June Platt Cook Book*, her three best-known books. She wrote for a number of other magazines as well, and in time became, I would say, a household necessity. People who appreciated recipes that were compact, easy to follow and foolproof grew into what we might call a "June Platt cult." I well remember being invited to dinners at which the host or hostess would say, with respect and not a little awe, "This is a June Platt recipe."

The recipe might have been American, French, Italian or pure June Platt. She is no gastronomic snob, thank heaven, but appreciates good food whatever its source. Our contemporary style of eating would be dull indeed without the influence of her forays into international cuisines and her variations on classic and early American themes. And now she has done a New England cookbook, the profit of long years of living in Little Compton, Rhode Island. As we might suspect, hers is no ordinary collection of rules, no catalog of recipes for cranberries, grunts and buckles. It contains only one recipe for baked beans, and that, unusual and good. She has delved into the lore of New England for a variety of excellent foods—some highly traditional and others so little known that she could not resist including them. As Mrs. Platt knows, the earliest cuisine of this region was frequently pretty uninspired, by necessity. However, the early settlers increased the supply of food, and ethnic groups adapted the food to their own backgrounds. Out of this came fascinating uses for native products. Especially memorable were the recipes for fish and shellfish, a testimony to the once bountiful supply found in New England waters. And it goes without saying that the seasons played an important part in the development of certain dishes. Mrs. Platt has sifted through the centuries of cookery and chosen her examples wisely. She has had the intelligence to realize that some of today's recipes are as distinctive as those used by the early Puritans, and these are included too. The result is a fascinating collection of regional Americana that covers over three hundred years.

For those who know June Platt and her work—and they must be legion by this time—the *New England Cook Book* will be a wonderful addition to the files. For those to whom Mrs. Platt is only a legend, this will provide a pleasant, intimate introduction to her personality and style. In either case, the reader will be rewarded with authentic knowledge and good eating.

JAMES BEARD

Contents

ONE

Soups & Chowders

DANIEL WEBSTER'S FISH CHOWDER

This, in his own words, is Daniel Webster's recipe for fish chowder, "suitable," he said, "for a large fishing party":

"Take a cod of ten pounds, well cleaned, leaving on the skin. Cut into pieces one and half pounds thick, preserving the head whole. Take one and a half pounds of clear, fat, salt pork, cut in thin slices. Do the same with twelve potatoes. Take the largest pot you have. Try out the pork first, then take out the pieces of pork, leaving in the drippings. Add to that three parts of water, a layer of fish, so as to the cover the bottom of the pot; next, a layer of potatoes, then two tablespoons of salt, 1 teaspoon of pepper, then the pork, another layer of fish, and the remainder of the potatoes.

"Fill the pot with water to cover the ingredients. Put it over a good fire, let the chowder boil twenty-five minutes. When this is done, have a quart of boiling milk ready, and ten hard crackers split and dipped in cold water. Add milk and crackers. Let the whole boil five minutes. The chowder is then ready and will be first-rate if you have followed the directions. An onion may be added if you like the flavor."

P.S. With all due respect to Daniel Webster, June Platt wouldn't like contending with the skin and bones.

SHRIMP-AND-FISH CHOWDER
(SERVES 4)

1 *pound fillet of cod or haddock*
½ *pound fresh shrimp*
2 *cups water*
Salt, pepper, and paprika to taste
3 *medium-size potatoes*
1 *one-inch square salt pork*
2 *small white onions*
1 *cup milk*
1 *cup heavy cream*

Rinse the fish and shrimp in cold water. Place in an enamel pan large enough to hold them comfortably. Pour over them the 2 cups water and season to taste with salt, pepper, and paprika. Bring gently to a simmer, skim, and cook about 15 minutes or until the fish flakes. Drain, saving the water. Shell the shrimp, clean, and put aside with the fish. Peel the potatoes and cut in cubes, add the fish-shrimp water, and cook until the potatoes are done. In the meantime dice the salt pork, peel the onions and slice thin. Sauté the pork and onions together until lightly browned; add these to the fish and shrimp in a deep aluminum pan, along with the drained potatoes. Cover with milk and cream and bring to the boiling point. Serve at once in hot soup plates. This is even better reheated the second day.

BAKED HADDOCK CHOWDER
(SERVES 6)

Preheat oven to 375°

    2 *large potatoes (1 pound)*
    3 *large yellow onions (¾ pound)*
    1 *pound haddock fillets*
    4 *tablespoons butter and more*
    Salt and pepper to taste
    1 *quart whole milk*
    Paprika
    12 *split and toasted Boston common crackers*

Butter the sides and bottom of a 3-quart oven-proof glass or enamel casserole. Wash and peel the potatoes; cut lengthwise in strips and then crosswise, making thin slices. Place temporarily in cold water. Peel the onions, quarter, and slice thin. Wash the fish and cut in bite-sized pieces, feeling carefully to be sure there are no bones. Drain the potatoes and place half of them in the buttered casserole, then add half the onions. Salt and pepper lightly, and dot generously with the butter. Cover with a thick layer of the fish, using all of it. Season again and butter generously. Add the remainder of the onions and top with the rest of the potatoes and use up the rest of the 4 tablespoons butter. Then pour in the quart of milk. Sprinkle lightly with paprika. Place the casserole, uncovered, in the preheated oven and bake for about 1¼ hours. The top by then should be a lovely golden brown, due to the paprika. Serve at once, accompanied by the heated crackers.

PUFFED BOSTON COMMON CRACKERS
(SERVES 6)

Preheat oven to 475–500°

> 12 *common crackers, split in two*
> 6 *tablespoons butter, well creamed*
> 1 *quart ice water*

Melt 1 tablespoon butter over low heat in a heavy iron frying pan. Set aside. Place the ice water in a shallow pan. Split the crackers and soak them in the ice water for about 2 to 3 minutes, turning them over once. Remove them from the water with a sieve spoon and drain for 5 minutes on several thicknesses of paper toweling. Place side by side in the buttered frying pan, round side down. Spread with the remaining 5 tablespoons butter. Place in the preheated oven and bake until they puff up, or for about 20 minutes. Turn them over carefully and cook about 5 minutes longer or until golden brown and crisp. Serve piping hot with chowder.

ELEANOR'S QUAHOG CHOWDER
(SERVES 4–6)

> 1 *3-inch square salt pork* (*more if desired*)
> 1 *large onion, sliced very thin*
> ½ *cup diced celery* (*optional*)
> ½ *stick butter*
> 1 *tablespoon flour*
> 1 *pint quahogs* (*they may be opened at the market*)
> 1 *cup potatoes cut in cubes or sliced very thin*
> 1 *quart milk* (*or half cream and half milk*)
> *Parsley*
> *Paprika*

Cut the pork into small cubes and try out on a very low flame. Cook the onion and celery very gently in the butter in a skillet and add the flour. Wash the quahogs very carefully in ¼ cup water. Be sure to remove all sand and shells. Strain and reserve this juice. Grind the quahogs in a food grinder, using the medium blade, or if using a chopping bowl, chop very fine. Cover the potatoes with the clam water and simmer. Do not cook them entirely, only partially. Skim carefully. Then add the butter-celery-onion mixture and chopped clams and cook 3 minutes. Do not boil. Scald the milk in a double boiler and add it to the clam mixture. Reheat the pork, pour off the extra fat, and scatter the crisp pork cubes on top of the chowder. Just before serving, garnish with parsley and paprika.

LOUISE'S QUAHOG CHOWDER
(SERVES 8)

2 *quarts quahogs in the shell, or 1 pint removed from the shells*
½ *pound lean salt pork washed and cut in ¼-inch cubes*
2 *large yellow onions, peeled and chopped fine*
2 *to 3 large potatoes, washed, peeled, and cut in ¼-inch cubes*
1½ *cups hot water*
Salt and freshly ground pepper to taste
1 *quart whole milk*
1 *pint all-purpose or heavy cream*
2 *tablespoons butter*
2 *cups oyster crackers or 8 Boston crackers*

This chowder differs considerably from Eleanor's. Louise, who is Portuguese, was brought up in Rhode Island and wouldn't think of buying the quahogs out of the shell. I'm afraid I'll settle for them shelled, having had a desperate time opening my first quahog (under Louise's expert tutelage), cracking and mutilating several before I finally opened one neatly, by balancing the shell (opening side up) on a wooden block, placing a sturdy knife in my left hand along the opening, and giving the knife a good whack with a heavy mallet. A proud moment for me when the shell split neatly open. I then scraped the poor quahog out with a fork into a bowl, saving almost every bit of clam juice. Nevertheless, I still recommend buying the quahogs shelled.

Louise started our chowder by first washing the quahogs one by one under running cold water. Then she opened them, and when they were all gathered together and in their juice in a bowl, she fished out the quahogs with a sieve spoon and strained the remaining juice through 2 thicknesses of clean cheesecloth, saving it, of course. This accomplished, she cut the salt pork with a sharp knife into tiny (¼-inch) cubes; peeled and chopped the onions very fine; washed and peeled the potatoes and cut them into ¼-inch cubes and covered them temporarily with cold water. She then put the clams themselves through the meat grinder, using the medium cutter, catching any juice in a bowl below.

Into my treasured large porcelain "oven-to-table" Dutch oven (bought with trading stamps) went the pork, to be rendered over medium heat until golden brown and crisp. These cubes were stirred constantly with a wooden spoon. In about 12 minutes they were just right. In went the chopped onions to be cooked until soft, or for about 8 minutes. About ¼ cup of the melted fat was removed and discarded. About ½ of the strained clam juice was added, plus 1 cup of the hot water; then the well-drained cubed potatoes went in, and the whole was gently cooked until the potatoes were tender (about 15–20 minutes), at which time the clams themselves and the remainder of their juice were added, along with the remaining ½ cup hot water, and the whole was allowed to cook gently for about 5 minutes longer. A very little salt was added, plus a sprinkle of freshly ground black pepper.

At this point, the resultant chowder base could have been allowed to cool completely and, when cold, placed in a freezer container to be frozen for a future treat. We, however, added a quart of whole milk and 2 tablespoons butter and stirred the chowder gently, until scalding hot, over a low heat. At the very last, the pint of heavy cream was added gradually, stirred carefully until very hot, but not allowed to boil, at which time the chowder was ready to serve, accompanied by toasted Boston common crackers or little oyster crackers.

CREAM OF CHICKEN SOUP
(SERVES 4–6)

3 *cups strong homemade chicken broth*
3 *egg yolks*
1 *cup heavy cream*
Fresh or dried dill (optional)
4–6 *tablespoons Marsala or sherry (optional)*

Heat the chicken broth in the top part of a double boiler. Beat together the egg yolks and heavy cream. Add slowly to the hot broth, stirring constantly, until the mixture coats the back of a spoon. Season with fresh or dried dill, and flavor with Marsala or sherry to taste.

SCOTCH BROSS
(SERVES 2)

1 *can water*
1 *can (10½ ounces) either condensed beef broth or consommé*
⅔ *cup quick-cooking Quaker oats (oatmeal)*
1 *teaspoon butter*

Add the can of water to the can of broth in a deep saucepan. Heat to the boiling point and gradually stir in the oatmeal. Cook, stirring constantly, until thickened, or for about 5 minutes. Remove from the heat, cover, and allow to stand 5 minutes. Reheat, stir in the butter, and serve in hot soup bowls.

NAVY-BEAN SOUP
(SERVES 6–8)

1 *pound (2 cups) dried navy beans*
4 *quarts cold water*
Hambone, about 1½ pounds, left over from home-baked ham
1 *carrot (peeled)*
2 *onions (peeled)*
2 *whole cloves*
4 *additional quarts cold water*
2 *cans (10½-ounce) beef broth (bouillon)*
Extra boiling water as needed
Buttered Croutons (see page 9)

The night before, pick over carefully and wash the beans. Place them in a large pot and cover with 4 quarts cold water. Cover and soak overnight. Likewise, the night before, place the hambone in another large pot, add the carrot, onions, and whole cloves and cover with another 4 quarts cold water. Bring gently to a boil, reduce heat, cover, and simmer gently for about 2 hours. Let stand overnight in a cool place.

The next morning drain the beans, discarding the water, and return the beans to a big pot. Strain the ham broth, discard the vegetables and hambone, and pour the broth over the beans. There should be about 3 quarts broth. Add extra boiling water if needed to make the 3 quarts. Cook the beans gently, skimming as necessary, until they are very tender, or for about 4 hours in all. It may be necessary to add another 2 or 3 cups boiling water to keep the beans well covered with broth. When they are done, remove from the fire and cool partially.

At this point put the whole through an electric blender to reduce to a fine purée. Then strain through a fine sieve to remove any roughage still remaining. When all this is done you should have about 6 cups of velvety purée which must be thinned with the contents of two cans of bouillon, giving you in all about 8 cups of bean soup. Serve scalding hot in a heated soup tureen and send to table accompanied by a bowl of crisp hot Buttered Croutons.

BUTTERED CROUTONS
Preheat oven to 425°–450° (optional)
6–8 slices white bread
¼ pound butter

Cut the bread with a sharp knife, making ½-inch cubes. Melt the butter in a shallow pan, add the cubes of bread, and stir constantly over low heat until a golden brown all over. Or you can stir lightly to butter all sides slightly, then place the pan in the preheated oven and watch carefully, until they are a light

golden brown, stirring or shaking them to brown all sides. Reheat before serving.

CORN CHOWDER
(SERVES 6)

*4 cups corn cut from cob, or 4 cups canned whole-kernel corn
(not cream-style)*
2 medium-size potatoes
1 small Bermuda onion (1 cup when chopped)
2½ cups water
2 cups clear chicken broth
5 tablespoons butter
2 cups hot milk
Salt and coarsely ground pepper to taste
Pinch cayenne
1 cup heavy cream

Cut the corn from the cobs, being careful not to cut too deep,
or use canned corn. Peel the potatoes and cut in ½-inch cubes.
Peel the Bermuda onion and chop fine. Place the corn in a large
(4-quart) pan. Pour over it 1 cup water and the chicken broth.
Place on low heat and simmer for 15 minutes, counting from the
time it comes to a boil. Watch carefully to prevent scorching.

In the meantime, boil the cubed potatoes in the remaining
1½ cups water until tender, or for about 15 minutes. Cook the
chopped Bermuda onion in 4 tablespoons butter, slowly, without browning, until soft, or for about 10 minutes. Add to the
corn the onion, well-drained potatoes, and hot milk. Put all this
mixture through the electric blender, a cup or two at a time,
running at low speed for 1 minute and another minute at high
speed. Place in the top of a very large double boiler. Season to
taste with salt and pepper and a dash of cayenne.

Place over boiling water and heat thoroughly. When the mixture is scalding hot, stir in the heavy cream. Place the remaining tablespoon butter in a soup tureen, pour over it the corn chowder and serve at once.

CREAM OF LEAF LETTUCE SOUP
(SERVES 6)
2 *cups finely chopped leaf lettuce*
3 *tablespoons butter*
2 *tablespoons flour*
1 *cup light cream*
3 *cups chicken broth*
Buttered Croutons (see page 9)

Wash plenty of tender leaf lettuce and chop sufficient of it very fine in a wooden bowl to yield 2 cups. Melt the butter in the top part of an enamel double boiler over low heat and stir in the flour, cook for a minute or two without burning, then gradually stir in the cream. Bring to a boil, stirring constantly, and simmer for 10 minutes. Add the chicken broth, bring to a boil again, and cook for another 10 minutes over low heat. Add the chopped lettuce and continue simmering for 10 minutes longer. Serve very hot in warm soup plates and garnish with Buttered Croutons.

COLD WATERCRESS-AND-POTATO SOUP
(SERVES 6–8)
2 *quarts water*
4 *small potatoes*
1 *large yellow onion*
1 *large bunch fresh watercress*

4 tablespoons butter
Salt to taste (about 1 tablespoon)
1 cup heavy or light cream

Heat the water. Wash and peel the potatoes and cut into medium-sized pieces. Peel and slice the onion fine. Wash the watercress; remove coarse stems and discard. Chop coarsely. Melt the butter in a large enamel pot, add the onion, and brown lightly, stirring constantly with a wooden spoon for about 6 minutes. Add the watercress, stir, and cook quickly for about 3 minutes. Add boiling water, salted to taste. Add the potatoes and cook gently for about 1 hour. Cool and put through a sieve, or run through an electric blender. Chill thoroughly and just before serving stir in the cream.

HOT OR COLD SORREL SOUP
(SERVES 6–8)

1 pint fresh sorrel leaves
3 large lettuce leaves, well washed
1 medium-size onion
½ teaspoon fresh or dried basil
½ teaspoon fresh or dried parsley or chervil
2 tablespoons butter
2 tablespoons flour
5 cups strong, clear chicken or beef broth
1 cup sour cream or 1¼ cups heavy sweet cream
4 egg yolks
Salt and pepper to taste

Wash the sorrel carefully and remove and discard the stems. Add the well-washed lettuce leaves and chop both together until very fine. This should make about 2 cups greens. Peel the onion and chop fine. Make a little cheesecloth bag and place in it the basil and chervil or parsley. Melt the butter in the top part of a 3-quart enamel double boiler over direct heat, add the onion and cook a minute or two without browning. Sprinkle with the flour, stir well, add the chopped greens and continue stirring a minute or two over low heat. Heat the broth and add it gradually to the greens. Add the herb bag, and cook until the greens are tender, about 10 minutes. Remove the herb bag.

To serve the soup hot, remove it from the fire and stir in gradually the cup of sour cream beaten together with the egg yolks. Season to taste with salt and pepper, and reheat over boiling water, stirring constantly.

To serve cold, beat together the sweet cream and egg yolks and stir gradually into the soup; cook over boiling water for about 3 minutes, stirring constantly; season to taste. Remove from the fire and cool, stirring occasionally. When cold refrigerate until very cold and serve garnished or not with a little sour cream.

PARSNIP CHOWDER
(SERVES 6–8)

5 *strips bacon*
1 *large yellow onion, peeled, cut in half, sliced very fine (1 cup)*
1½ *pounds parsnips, peeled, cored, and cut in ½-inch cubes*
   (3 cups)
1½ *pounds new potatoes, peeled and cut in ½-inch cubes*
   (3½ cups)
2 *cups boiling water*
3 *cups whole milk*

3 tablespoons butter
About 1 tablespoon salt
About ¼ teaspoon cracked black pepper
½ pint (1 cup) heavy cream
1 tablespoon finely chopped parsley

Fry the bacon gently until almost crisp (takes about 5 minutes). Remove the bacon and set aside on a paper towel. Add the onion to the remaining fat in the frying pan, and cook gently until soft but only lightly browned, or for about 5 minutes. Lift them from the pan with a sieve spoon and place them in a large enamel casserole. Add the parsnips and potatoes to the casserole and cover with the 2 cups boiling water. Cover the casserole and cook about ½ hour until the vegetables are tender. When they are done, add the milk and bring to boiling point. Stir in the butter and leftover bacon fat, season to taste. Set aside until you are ready to heat and serve.

When the soup is scalding hot, stir in gradually the heavy cream; place in a heated soup tureen. Sprinkle with the bacon, which you have cut in tiny pieces with scissors and heated carefully in a separate small frying pan. Sprinkle also with chopped parsley, and send to the table to be ladled into hot soup plates. With this serve heated, split Boston common crackers or pilot wafers.

LITTLE COMPTON VEGETABLE SOUP
(MAKES 4½ QUARTS)

½ peck (4 quarts, about 28) juicy red tomatoes
3 large yellow onions (about 1 pound)
2 large green peppers
1 bunch celery

3 *tablespoons butter*
¾ *cup granulated sugar*
1 *tablespoon salt*
1 *bay leaf*
1 *quart boiling water*
Extra butter

First, dip the tomatoes one by one into boiling water, then into cold, and remove the skins. Slice the tomatoes crosswise in two and scoop out the seeds, putting the seeds apart temporarily. Now cut or chop the tomatoes coarsely, and place in a large enamel pan. Next peel and slice the onions fine, cutting the slices again into quarters. Set them aside. Wash the peppers and remove the stems; cut in two lengthwise, discard the seeds, and cut lengthwise in ¼-inch strips, then cut the strips crosswise, making small squares. Pull the celery stalks apart, wash carefully, remove and discard the leaves, break the stalks backward in half, and remove the threads. This is important. Now cut the celery lengthwise in strips and again crosswise, making squares like the peppers.

Now cook the onions and peppers in the butter, over low heat, until limp but not browned, or for about 10 minutes. Add them to the tomatoes. Strain the tomato seeds, adding the juice to the tomatoes. Discard the seeds of the tomatoes. Add the celery, sugar, salt, bay leaf, and boiling water. Bring the whole to a boil, stirring occasionally, and simmer gently for 2 hours, skimming frequently.

When the soup is done, place a lump of butter in a hot soup tureen, and add the required number of cups of the soup (allowing 1 cup per person) and serve piping hot at the table. Pour the rest of the soup when completely cold into freezing containers and place in a deep freeze or in the freezing compartment of the refrigerator for future use.

AUDREY'S PEA SOUP
(SERVES 8)

6 *large leeks*
2 *white onions*
¼ *pound butter*
4 *cans* (12½-ounce) *clear chicken broth*
1½-pound *bag frozen peas*
2 *cups light or all-purpose cream*
Salt and freshly ground pepper to taste
Chopped chives (optional) *if served cold*

Remove the outer leaves and the green part of the leeks, and split down the center. Wash thoroughly to remove all the sand. Peel the onions. Chop the leeks and onions fine. Melt the butter slowly over low heat in a large enamel pan, add the leeks and onions, and cook gently until limp, stirring constantly with a wooden spoon, adding a spoonful of water as necessary to prevent browning. This will take about 15 minutes, so don't hurry it. In the meantime open the cans of chicken broth and heat to the boiling point. Add this to the vegetables and cook 10 minutes longer before adding the frozen peas, a few at a time, so that the broth boils constantly. Simmer about 20 minutes or until the peas are tender. Remove from the heat and cool partially. Put the whole (a cupful and a half at a time) through an electric blender, counting 50 for each lot. This will give you about 8 cups of base, which may be used right away or put into freezer containers and frozen for future use.

When you are ready to serve, place the base in the top part

of a large double boiler over hot water until it is scalding hot, then add the cream gradually, stirring constantly, until very hot. Never let it boil, once the cream has been added. Taste and add a bit of salt if necessary and a dash of pepper.

This soup is equally good served ice cold, garnished or not with a few chopped chives. It should be thawed when taken from the freezer and thinned with the cream.

CHESTNUT SOUP
(SERVES 6–8)

1 *quart large French chestnuts*
1 *teaspoon granulated sugar*
1 *teaspoon salt*
6–8 *thin strips of peel cut from a lemon, minus white part*
2 *quarts strong, well-seasoned clear chicken broth*
1 *tablespoon cornstarch, moistened with*
1 *tablespoon cold water*
1 *generous tablespoon butter*

Wash the chestnuts in hot water, place in a large pan, and cover with cold water. Boil about 20 minutes. Peel, one by one, rinsing each as you go along in cold water to avoid burnt fingers, leaving the others in the hot water. When all are peeled and the inner skins have been removed, place in another saucepan and cover with cold water, add the sugar, salt, and lemon peel and bring to a boil. Cook until the chestnuts are very tender, or for about 15 to 20 minutes. Remove the lemon peel and place what juice remains and the nuts in an electric blender and run until smooth, counting to about 50. Place in a deep pan and add the chicken broth; boil gently for about another 15 minutes, skimming carefully as it cooks. Moisten the cornstarch with the water, stir until smooth, add to the soup, and cook for a minute or two longer or until the soup is thickened and smooth. Add the butter just before serving piping hot.

CORNMEAL CRISPS
(MAKES 3 TO 4 DOZEN)

Preheat oven to 475°–500°

> 1 *cup white water-ground cornmeal*
> 1 *cup all-purpose flour, unsifted*
> ½ *teaspoon salt and more*
> 1 *tablespoon granulated sugar*
> 3 *teaspoons baking powder*
> 2 *eggs*
> 1½ *cups milk*
> 5 *tablespoons melted butter and more*

Butter copiously 3 or 4 large cookie sheets. Sift together into a bowl the cornmeal, flour, salt, sugar, and baking powder. Beat the eggs, add the milk, and stir into the dry ingredients, mixing with a spoon until smooth and free from lumps. A few turns with a rotary beater will help, but don't overbeat. Stir in the 5 tablespoons melted butter. Drop the batter by small tablespoonfuls onto the cookie sheets, spreading it as thin as possible in 3-to-3½-inch circles, placing them not too close together, as they spread a little while baking. If your oven has 3 racks, so much the better, as ideally these should be cooked immediately after mixing.

Place the pans in the preheated oven and bake until the cornmeal crisps begin to brown around the edges, at which time remove them from the oven, loosen them from the pan with a spatula, and return the pans to the oven until the cakes are lightly browned almost to the center, or cook 15 to 20 minutes in all. Remove from the pans immediately and place on cookie racks to cool. Store in an air-tight container, and when you are ready to serve, brush them lightly with melted butter, sprinkle lightly with salt, and reheat in a hot oven. Serve with soup or cocktails.

KATHERINE'S CHEESE STICKS
(32 STICKS)

Preheat oven to 325°–350°

    1 *cup all-purpose flour*

    ¼ *teaspoon cayenne pepper*

    ¼ *teaspoon salt*

    ⅔ *cup freshly grated imported Parmesan cheese*

    ¼ *pound* (1 *bar*) *salted butter at room temperature*

    ⅛ *cup milk or cream*

Sift flour, cayenne, and salt into a bowl. Add the cheese and soft butter. Work with your fingertips until the mixture becomes a dough that will just hold together. Gather the dough into a ball, and roll out on a lightly floured pastry cloth or board, making a rectangle ½-inch thick, 5 inches wide, and 8 inches long. Cut this lengthwise through the center, then crosswise in ½-inch strips, making 32 bars in all. Paint these lightly with a finger dipped in cream or milk. Place neatly in regimental rows on a cookie sheet, far enough apart so that they don't touch each other. Place in a preheated oven and bake until they are a light golden brown, or for about 20 to 25 minutes. When cool, place in a covered tin until you are ready to serve them with cocktails.

Note: These may be made substituting grated American cheese for the Parmesan, but they are a little more fragile, so loosen them gently from the pan while still hot.

Very good with soup or cocktails.

TWO

Fish & Seafood

POACHED SALMON WITH HARD-BOILED-EGG
CREAM SAUCE
(SERVES 6–8)

It is a tradition in New England to serve Poached Salmon with
Hard-Boiled-Egg Cream Sauce, along with the first boiled new
potatoes and early fresh green peas, on the Fourth of July.

5-pound piece fresh salmon (preferably from the center of the
 fish)
Fresh parsley
2 lemons, quartered
Capers, well drained

DRY-WHITE-WINE COURT BOUILLON
Warm water to cover the fish
1 cup dry white wine

1 *teaspoon salt*
2 *carrots, peeled and sliced*
A *little parsley*
2 *tablespoons cider vinegar*
1 *large peeled, sliced onion*

FOR THE SAUCE
4 *hard-boiled eggs*
6 *tablespoons butter*
6 *tablespoons flour*
2 *cups rich hot milk*
Salt and pepper to taste
½ *cup heavy cream*

Make the court bouillon, simmering it for 15 to 30 minutes. Wrap the salmon in a piece of cheesecloth and tie the ends with string. Place in a fish boiler and cover completely with warm (not hot) court bouillon. Place on the fire, bring slowly to the simmering point, and simmer for about 50 minutes.

In the meantime, make some Hard-Boiled-Egg Cream Sauce. Place the eggs in a pan and cover with cold water. Place on the fire and bring slowly to the boiling point, reduce heat, and boil the eggs gently for 15 minutes. Plunge the eggs into cold water for a few minutes, then crack and remove the shells.

Now make the sauce. Place the butter in the top part of a double boiler. Melt the butter and add the flour. Cook together for a second or two, stirring constantly with a wooden spoon, then gradually add the hot milk to make a thick, smooth sauce. Cut the hard-boiled eggs lengthwise, making 6 slices each. Season the cream sauce to taste with salt and pepper, and thin to the desired thickness with the cream. Place over boiling water and fold in the sliced eggs. Cover and keep warm, while you remove the fish from the fish boiler.

Place it on a hot fish platter and cut off the ends of the cheesecloth and spread out the cheesecloth. Now, working quickly, remove all the skin from the top side of the salmon. Lift one side of the cheesecloth and roll the fish over onto the other side, removing the cheesecloth as you do so. Remove the rest of the skin and decorate the fish platter with plenty of parsley and quartered lemons. Send to the table accompanied by the Hard-Boiled-Egg Cream Sauce and a separate little bowl of capers.

CRAB SUPREME
(8 SHELLS)

Preheat broiling unit to 450°

6 hard-cooked eggs or fewer
3 cups crabmeat
½ teaspoon dry mustard
1 teaspoon grated onion
1 cup mayonnaise
Scant ¼ cup dry sherry
1½ cups rolled Ritz crackers
4 tablespoons butter
2 tablespoons chopped parsley

Hard-boil the eggs and cool. Remove the shells and chop the eggs coarsely. Drain the crabmeat thoroughly, break it apart with a fork, and place in a bowl. Add the mustard and onion to the mayonnaise. Thin with sherry. Pour over the crabmeat. Fold in the eggs. Heat the crackers in the oven until crisp, then roll or crush them coarsely. Place the crabmeat in 8 large lightly buttered scallop shells, distributing it equally. Sprinkle with crumbs and dot with butter. Place under the broiler unit about 4 inches below the heat. Broil until just heated through and lightly browned. Sprinkle with chopped parsley and serve at once.

DEVILED CRABMEAT
(SERVES 4)

Preheat oven to 400°

> 1 cup crabmeat (about ¼ pound)
> 1 slice white bread, crusts removed
> ½ cup boiling water
> 4 tablespoons butter
> 2 tablespoons heavy cream
> ¼ teaspoon salt
> Dash of pepper
> ¼ teaspoon cayenne
> ¼ teaspoon dry mustard
> 1 teaspoon Worcestershire sauce
> 14 stuffed olives, chopped fine
> ¼ cup dry bread crumbs
> 1 tablespoon chopped parsley

Pick the crabmeat over carefully and remove any bits of shell encountered. Set crabmeat aside in a bowl. Break the bread into small pieces, and pour over it the boiling water. Add 1 tablespoon of the butter and the cream. Season with the salt, pepper, cayenne, dry mustard, and Worcestershire sauce. Add the chopped olives and the crabmeat. Mix well and place in 4 buttered scallop shells. Melt the remaining 3 tablespoons butter in a small frying pan and stir in the dry bread crumbs. When the crumbs are heated through, cover the mixture in the shells, distributing crumbs equally. Place in the preheated oven and bake until lightly browned on top, or for about 15 minutes. Sprinkle with the parsley and serve piping hot.

CRABMEAT-STUFFED BAKED SWEET GREEN PEPPERS
(SERVES 6)

Preheat oven to 375°

> 3 *large green peppers*
> ½ *pound fresh crabmeat*
> 3 *hard-boiled eggs*
> ¼ *teaspoon salt*
> *Dash of pepper*
> ½ *teaspoon paprika*
> 2 *tablespoons parsley*
> ¾ *cups or more light cream*
> ½ *cup dry bread crumbs*
> 6 *tablespoons butter*

Wash the peppers, cut in half lengthwise, and remove the seeds. Parboil 10 minutes in boiling lightly salted water. Drain and pat dry. Place in a lightly buttered baking dish. Look the crabmeat over carefully and discard any sharp bits encountered. Chop the eggs coarsely and add to the crab. Season with the salt, pepper, paprika, and parsley. Fill the peppers with the mixture and pour into each half about 2 tablespoons of the cream. Sprinkle each with the crumbs, and dot with the butter. Bake for about 10 minutes, basting once or twice with a little additional cream. When bubbling hot, serve at once.

LOBSTER PATTIES
(SERVES 4)

1 *cup cooked lobster meat*
2 *tablespoons butter*
3 *tablespoons flour*
½ *cup light cream*
¼ *teaspoon grated nutmeg*
Generous pinch of cayenne
Salt to taste
Yolk of 1 egg
1 *whole egg*
2 *tablespoons water*
1 *cup fine toasted bread crumbs*
1 *can (14-ounce) vegetable shortening*

Chop the lobster meat fine. Make a thick cream sauce using the butter, flour, and light cream. Add the lobster and season highly to taste with the nutmeg, cayenne, and about ½ teaspoon salt. Stir in the slightly beaten egg yolk. Spread in a well-buttered shallow dish. Refrigerate for several hours, or until you are ready to shape the patties and French-fry them.

Beat the whole egg together with 2 tablespoons water. In a separate shallow dish, place a heaping cup of toasted bread crumbs. Shape the lobster mixture into 8 small patties, about ½ inch thick. Roll the patties in crumbs, dip into the beaten egg and water and roll again in crumbs. In a deep heavy iron or aluminum pan heat the contents of a 14-ounce can of vegetable shortening until hot but not smoking, or until it registers 375° on a fat thermometer. To test without a thermometer, drop a small piece of bread into the fat, and if it is golden brown in about 50 seconds, the fat is the correct temperature. Drop the patties into the fat and fry until they are a deep brown or for about 4 to 5 minutes, turning them over once with a perforated spoon. Place them on a paper towel and keep warm in the oven until you are ready to serve, which should be as soon as possible. Serve with Creamed Herb Sauce.

CREAMED HERB SAUCE
(SERVES 6)

4 shallots, peeled and chopped fine
1 tablespoon butter
1 tablespoon flour
1 cup hot milk
2 egg yolks
½ cup heavy cream
Salt and freshly ground pepper to taste
Grated rind of 1 lemon
1 tablespoon chopped parsley or chervil
4 dozen tarragon leaves, cut fine
Juice of 1 lemon (strained)

Chop the shallots very fine and cook them slowly in the butter in the top of a double boiler over direct heat, being careful not to brown them at all; add the flour; cook together a minute or two, then gradually add the boiling milk. When the mixture is smooth and slightly thickened, place over boiling water; cook a while longer. When ready to serve, beat the egg yolks with the cream and stir into them a little of the hot sauce, then add the eggs to the cream sauce gradually and continue cooking over boiling water, stirring constantly, until the sauce is thickened. Season to taste with salt and pepper, then add the grated lemon rind, being sure not to include any of the white part, which would give the sauce a bitter taste. At the last add the chopped parsley or chervil, the cut tarragon leaves, and the strained lemon juice.

Serve with Lobster Patties, boiled fish, boiled cauliflower, string beans, or boiled chicken.

LOBSTER NEWBURG
(SERVES 6)

2 *cups cooked lobster meat, cut in medium chunks*
2 *tablespoons dry sherry*
¼ *pound butter*
1 *tablespoon flour*
5 *egg yolks*
2 *cups all-purpose cream*
½ *cup milk*
Salt and freshly ground pepper to taste
6 *slices white bread, crusts removed, toasted, cut into triangles*

Place the lobster meat in the top part of an enamel double boiler, add the sherry and place over hot water to warm. Melt the butter in a small pan on low heat and blend in the flour. Set aside. Beat the egg yolks slightly and stir in the cream and milk. When well mixed, place in the top part of another double boiler over boiling water and cook, stirring constantly, until hot but not yet thickened. Stir in the butter and flour gradually, add the lobster and sherry and stir constantly over boiling water until the mixture is thick and smooth and hot. Season to taste with about ⅓ teaspoon salt and a dash of pepper. Serve immediately on hot freshly toasted triangles of bread.

STEAMED CLAMS (with Broth)
(SERVES 6)

4 quarts medium-sized fresh steamer clams
2 cups cold water
½ pound butter (melted)
Strained juice of 1 lemon
Salt and pepper to taste

With a small brush, kept for the purpose, scrub the clams thoroughly one by one under cold running water, to remove all the sand. Put the clams into the upper section of an enamel steamer sold for the purpose. Put the cold water into the bottom section. Cover and cook over low to moderate heat, steaming the clams until they open way out, about 15 to 20 minutes, counting from the time they start actually steaming.

Place the clams in a large bowl, and serve with individual dishes of hot melted butter to which has been added the strained lemon juice and salt and pepper to taste. To eat, remove from the shells, one by one, and dip into the seasoned butter, and eat all but the neck or syphon. Allow the liquor in the lower section of steamer to settle, and serve the broth in cups, allowing it to drain off by way of the little spigot provided for the purpose on the lower part of the steamer.

MOTHER CROSS'S CLAM PIE
(SERVES 6)

Preheat oven to 475°
FOR THE PASTRY

2 cups pastry flour
½ teaspoon salt

⅓ *cup butter*
⅓ *cup vegetable shortening*
About ⅓ *cup ice water*

First mix the pastry. Sift the flour with the salt. Work in the shortenings with a pastry cutter or your fingers. Stir with a fork and moisten with ice water to make a dough. Shape gently into two flat balls, one slightly larger than the other. Wrap in waxed paper and chill until you have mixed and cooled the filling.

FOR THE FILLING

4 *cans* (7½-*ounce*) *minced clams*
4 *ounces salt pork*
1 *tablespoon butter*
2 *tablespoons flour*
Pepper to taste

Slice the salt pork thin and cut in ½-inch squares. Open the four cans of clams and drain, but save the juice. Try out the pork gently in a heavy pan, stirring with a wooden spoon to prevent burning. Add the butter; blend in the flour, cook for a minute or two without browning, then gradually add the juice from the clams. Cook until thickened, or for a minute or two. Add pepper to taste and the clams, and simmer, stirring frequently, for about 10 to 15 minutes. Set aside to cool.

When ready to assemble and bake the pie, roll out the larger ball of pastry to a size large enough to cover a 9-inch pie plate, with about a ¾-inch overhang. Ease into the pie plate. Fill with the cooled clams. Roll out the smaller piece of pastry to a circle large enough to cover the pie, with a ¾-inch overhang. Moisten the edge of the lower crust, and cover the pie with the second crust. Press the edges together and crimp prettily. Cut out a hole in the center of the pie, about the size of a 50-cent piece. Roll out the leftover scraps of pastry and make a 3-by-1-inch wide strip. Roll this around three fingers to form a rose for the center of the pie. Insert this in the center hole, leaving plenty of room for the steam to escape. Bake in the preheated hot oven for 15 minutes or until the pie begins to brown, then decrease heat to 375°–400° and continue baking about 20 minutes longer. Serve piping hot.

BROILED BAY SCALLOPS
(SERVES 4–6)

Preheat broiler

> 1–1½ *pounds bay scallops*
> 2 *tablespoons vinegar*
> ¼ *teaspoon each salt and freshly ground pepper*
> 6 *tablespoons olive oil*
> ⅔ *cup toasted fine bread crumbs*
> 1 *tablespoon chopped parsley*

Marinate the scallops in a dressing made of the vinegar, salt, pepper and olive oil for 15 minutes. Drain and roll the scallops in fine bread crumbs. Spread out on an oiled foil-lined pan, place under the broiling unit, approximately 3 inches below the heat, and cook 13–15 minutes, or until they are golden brown all over. Shake the pan occasionally while cooking to brown the scallops evenly. Sprinkle with chopped parsley and serve with Tartar Sauce, or melted butter and lemon wedges.

TARTAR SAUCE
(SERVES 6)

1 *cup mayonnaise*
1 *teaspoon finely chopped shallots*
1 *teaspoon well-chopped parsley*
½ *teaspoon chopped onion*
2 *teaspoons chopped capers (packed in vinegar, not salt)*
2 *teaspoons chopped pickle*

To the mayonnaise, add all the other ingredients. Mix well.

BAY SCALLOPS NEWBURG
(SERVES 4)

2 *cups (1 pound) small bay scallops*
4 *tablespoons (½ bar) butter*
½ *teaspoon fresh paprika*
⅓ *teaspoon nutmeg*
3 *egg yolks*
1 *cup heavy cream*
¼ *cup dry sherry*
Salt to taste
8 *triangles of toast, buttered*

Wash the scallops and drain well. Melt the butter in the top part of a double boiler over boiling water. Add the scallops and cook, stirring occasionally, for about 5 or 6 minutes. Add the paprika and nutmeg and cook about 1 minute longer. Beat together the egg yolks and cream and pour over the scallops. Cook, stirring constantly, until well thickened, or for about 7 or 8 minutes longer. Remove from the heat, stir in the sherry, and season to taste. Serve at once on lightly buttered toast.

BROILED BAY SCALLOPS
(MAKES 24)

Preheat broiling unit

> *¼ pound (about 24) fresh small bay scallops*
> *4 strips bacon, cut in half lengthwise*
> *Toothpicks*

Wash the scallops in cold water and pat dry on paper toweling. Cut the 8 strips of bacon crosswise in three parts, making 24 pieces in all. Wrap each scallop in a piece of the bacon and place in an oven-proof shallow pan or baking dish. Place under the preheated broiler, about 3 inches below the unit. Broil until the bacon is a golden brown, or for about 20 minutes. Spear each one with a toothpick and serve, while still hot, with cocktails. If desired for a fish course for 4, double the recipe and serve right in the dish in which the scallops were cooked, but omit the toothpicks.

LOUISE'S CODFISH CAKES
(18 FISH CAKES; SERVES 6)

> *6 ounces salt codfish*
> *3 large potatoes (1½ pounds)*
> *1½ pounds vegetable fat*
> *2 eggs*
> *Salt and pepper to taste*

Wash the fish in cold water. Bring to a boil in fresh cold water. Drain, cover with fresh cold water and bring to a boil again. Repeat this 6 times in all. Drain once more, cover with fresh water, and boil until the fish flakes apart, or for about 45 minutes. In the meantime wash and peel the potatoes, and cut into 8 parts each. Cook the potatoes in a heavy aluminum saucepan until very tender, drain, and add the well-drained fish. Beat with a portable electric beater until light and smooth, then beat in the eggs one at a time.

Have ready a deep aluminum saucepan equipped with a fat thermometer, and place in it the vegetable fat.

Heat the fat to frying temperature, 370°. Salt and pepper the fish-and-potato mixture to taste, and drop by tablespoonfuls into the hot fat, making not more than 6 at a time. When they are a golden brown on one side, roll gently over onto the other side, using a sieve spoon. In about 5 minutes the cakes should be done to a turn. Drain on several thicknesses of paper toweling and repeat the process, making about 18 cakes in all. Serve at once, or place in a hot serving dish and keep warm in a moderately hot oven until ready to serve.

BACALHAU OR SALT COD À LA PORTUGAISE
(SERVES 6)

1 *pound choice boneless salt codfish*
4 *large ripe tomatoes, peeled, quartered, and sliced crosswise*
4 *large yellow onions, peeled, quartered, and sliced crosswise*
2 *large potatoes, peeled, quartered, and sliced crosswise*
2 *4-ounce glasses of fine-roasted pimientos (chopped)*
2 *teaspoons butter*
Salt and pepper to taste
2 *tablespoons olive oil*

Wash the fish, cover with cold water, and soak for 12 hours, changing the water frequently. When ready to cook, drain, and cover once more with fresh water. Place on very low heat and bring very slowly to a simmer. Do not allow to boil. Skim carefully and continue simmering until the fish may be easily pulled apart into large flakes with a fork, or for about ½ hour. Remove from heat and drain well.

Prepare the tomatoes, onions, potatoes, and pimientos, and using 1 teaspoon of the butter, butter the sides and bottom of a large deep earthenware or enamel-lined casserole. Starting with part of the tomatoes, arrange all the ingredients in alternate layers, adding salt and pepper to each layer to taste, ending up with tomatoes. Dot with the remaining teaspoon of butter and trickle the olive oil over all. Cover the casserole tightly and bring very slowly to a simmer, over very low heat. Simmer until the potatoes and fish are tender, or for about 1½ hours. Serve in hot soup plates, accompanied by toasted and well-buttered English muffins or Portuguese bread.

BAKED BLUEFISH
(SERVES 4–6)

Preheat oven to 400°

> 3- to 4-pound bluefish
> 4 ounces fresh salt pork
> Salt and freshly ground pepper to taste
> 3 tablespoons butter
> 1 cup milk or more
> 1 teaspoon chopped parsley

Ask the fish man to split and clean the fish, removing the head and tail and backbone. Wash it carefully in cold water, and pat dry with paper toweling. Slice the salt pork in thin pieces and lay it on a shallow baking dish, large enough to hold the fillets. Lay the fish skin side down on the salt pork, sprinkle with salt and pepper, dot with the butter and pour over the fish the cup of milk, or more if necessary to completely cover the bottom of the baking dish. Bake for about 45 minutes, basting occasionally. Sprinkle with parsley and serve on hot plates accompanied by buttered boiled new potatoes.

BROILED FRESH SWORDFISH WITH BUTTER AND WORCESTERSHIRE SAUCE
(SERVES 6–8)

Preheat broiler to 375°

> *4 pounds fresh swordfish cut 1½ inches thick*
> *½ pound butter at room temperature*
> *½ teaspoon salt*
> *¼ teaspoon coarsely ground pepper*
> *2 lemons (quartered)*

SAUCE

> *⅜ pound butter*
> *3 tablespoons Worcestershire sauce*

Line a shallow broiling pan, 14 inches by 10 inches by 1¼ inches deep, with aluminum foil. Grease the foil with 2 tablespoons of the soft butter. Place the swordfish on the foil. Spread with the remaining 6 tablespoons soft butter, and sprinkle with salt and pepper. Place the pan 3 inches from the broiling unit, and broil the fish slowly for 35 to 45 minutes, or until opaque through, basting frequently with the butter drippings. Increase heat to 450° the last five minutes to brown the fish well.

Lift carefully onto a hot platter, pouring drippings over the fish, garnish with the lemons and the sauce (made by melting the butter in a saucepan, then adding Worcestershire sauce, and heating both together for a few seconds).

Serve with boiled new potatoes.

BAKED SWORDFISH
(SERVES 6–8)

Preheat oven to 400°

 3 to 4 pounds fresh swordfish, cut 1½ inches thick
 Salt and pepper to taste
 2 tablespoons soft butter
 1 cup coarse toasted bread crumbs
 About 2 cups milk
 2 lemons, quartered
 1 tablespoon chopped parsley

Wash the fish in cold water, and wipe dry on paper toweling. Place in a lightly buttered oven-proof rectangular dish, large enough to hold it comfortably. Salt and pepper it lightly. Rub the soft butter into the bread crumbs, and sprinkle evenly over the fish. Pour the milk around the fish to half cover it. Place in a preheated hot oven to bake about 30 to 40 minutes, basting frequently with the hot milk surrounding it. Garnish with quartered lemons, sprinkle with parsley, and serve at once.

BROILED NEW ENGLAND SCROD
(SERVES 6)

 3–3½-pound scrod (young cod or haddock)
 Salt and pepper to taste
 3–4 tablespoons olive oil
 2 tablespoons melted butter

Juice of ½ lemon
1 teaspoon chopped parsley or fresh tarragon

Have the scrod split and cleaned and the backbone removed without separating the halves. Have the head and tail removed. Wipe as dry as possible, sprinkle with salt and pepper and let stand overnight in the refrigerator. When you are ready to cook, preheat the broiling unit of the stove. Line a broiling pan with aluminum foil, rub the foil with olive oil, place the fish skin side down on the foil. Sprinkle the fish with the remaining olive oil. Cook under the broiling unit 2 inches from the heat for about 15 minutes or until the fish flakes when tried with a fork. Transfer the fish to a hot platter flesh side up, and pour over it the melted butter mixed with lemon juice and parsley or tarragon. Serve on hot plates with creamed or hashed-brown potatoes.

BAKED HALIBUT
(SERVES 4)

Preheat oven to 400°

1½-pound slice halibut
Salt and pepper to taste
1 large ripe tomato, peeled
½ large green pepper
6 tablespoons butter

Wash the fish in cold water, pat dry, and cut away the skin around the edges. Place on a well-buttered shallow oven-proof baking dish, large enough to hold it comfortably. Sprinkle with pepper and salt. Peel the tomato and slice thin. Cover the fish with the tomato. Wash a green pepper, cut in half, and slice one half very fine, first removing the seeds. Cover the tomatoes with the pepper, and dot with butter. Place in the preheated oven and bake for 25 minutes, basting once or twice with the juice in the dish. Serve on hot plates.

CREAMED SMOKED HADDOCK
(SERVES 4)

Preheat oven to 350°

> 1 *pound smoked haddock*
> 3 *medium-sized onions*
> 4 *tablespoons butter and more*
> 1 *cup or more heavy cream*

Wash the haddock and dry well on a paper towel. Place in a well-buttered enamel or oven-proof glass dish. Peel the onions, cut them in half, and slice very thin. Sauté these separately in a saucepan in the butter, without browning, until transparent. Spread on top of the fish. Bake uncovered in the preheated oven for 55 minutes, at which time add 1 cup heavy cream and cook about 5 minutes longer, or until thick and creamy. Serve at once, accompanied by boiled white potatoes and buttered fresh green peas. The fish may be cooked ahead of time and set aside until you are ready to serve, at which time add a little more cream, and reheat until bubbling hot, either in the oven or on top of the stove.

SALMON À LA REINE
(SERVES 6)

1 *can (1 pound) salmon or, better still, boiled fresh salmon, minus all skin and bones*

4 *tablespoons butter*
2 *tablespoons flour*
1 *cup boiling water*
Salt and pepper to taste
2 *small grated onions*
Juice of 1 lemon
4 *hard-boiled eggs*
1 *tablespoon chopped parsley or fresh dill*
Cooked rice

Look the cooked salmon over carefully, removing all skin and bones. Melt the butter in the top part of a large double boiler on low direct heat, and stir in the flour, with a wooden spoon. Cook for a minute or two, then gradually add the boiling water, making a smooth sauce. Season to taste with salt and pepper, add the grated onions and lemon juice, and cook for a little while over boiling water (about 5 minutes). Add the salmon, stirring lightly with a fork, and continue cooking about 5 minutes longer. In the meantime, remove the cooked yolks from the eggs and rub them through a fine sieve. Stir them into the fish. Slice the whites and add them also to the fish. Place in a hot serving dish, sprinkle with chopped dill or parsley, and serve at once over fluffy hot rice.

THREE

Poultry & a Few Egg Dishes

PARTRIDGE OR CHICKEN NEW HAMPSHIRE STYLE
(SERVES 4–6)

4 heaping cups dried marrow beans
1 partridge or one 4½- to 5-pound fowl
1 pound lean salt pork
4 small white onions, peeled
1 teaspoon dry mustard
1½ teaspoons salt
2 generous tablespoons molasses
½ cup hot water

Wash and pick over the beans and soak overnight. The next morning, drain off the water in which they have soaked, cover them with fresh water, heat slowly, and cook, keeping below the boiling point, until the skins burst when you take some on a spoon and blow on them. Don't overcook.

Now, if you happen to be the proud possessor of a fine plump partridge, clean and truss it with care. If not, do the same to a 4½- to 5-pound fowl. Also cover the lean salt pork with water, bring to a boil and drain; cut it into 4 pieces, each piece scored in several places. Place the bird in the bottom of a large iron pot, or in an earthenware cocotte. Drain the beans, but save the water. Put the onions in the pot, then cover the bird and onions with the beans. Make a paste of the dry mustard, salt, and molasses, stir in the ½ cup hot water, and pour the whole over the beans. Tuck the four pieces of scalded salt pork down into the beans, scored side up. Then add enough of the bean water to completely cover the beans, partridge, and pork.

Cover tightly, place in a 300° oven, and bake slowly, without stirring, at least 6 or 7 hours. Every half hour or so add a little boiling water so that the beans do not dry out. Fifteen minutes before serving, remove the cover and allow the beans to brown. Tie a large napkin around the pot and serve at once as it is. The chicken or partridge remains whole, but the meat falls from the bones at the slightest touch, so with a little care it is possible to serve each person a bit of the bird, minus bones, along with the beans and the pork.

P.S. A lumberjack's technique would be to put a heavy piece of paper over the pot before adjusting the lid; then he would proceed to cook the beans by burying the pot in a deep hole lined with hot stones and red-hot hardwood ashes. He would then cover the pot with 1½ feet more of red-hot ashes, then with a thick covering of dead ashes, so that no more smoke could be seen. All this would be at 4 o'clock in the afternoon, and not until the next morning would the beans be eaten. My method will be found infinitely simpler.

CHICKEN FRICASSEE
(SERVES 4)

2 *large whole chicken breasts (about 1 pound each)*
1 *large carrot, peeled*
1 *large stalk celery, washed*
Pinch of white pepper
½ *teaspoon salt*
1 *cup water*
1 *can (13¾-ounce) chicken broth*
2 *tablespoons butter*
3 *tablespoons all-purpose flour*
½ *cup heavy cream*
1 *tablespoon chopped parsley*

Wash the chicken breasts, dry, and singe if necessary. Place in a large pan, add the carrot and celery, pepper, salt, water, and chicken broth. Bring slowly to a simmer, skim carefully, cover partially, and cook gently until the chicken is tender, or for about 1½ hours. Cool partially, then remove all the skin and bones, leaving the pieces of breast as whole as possible, placing them back in the broth.

Now make the sauce. Melt the butter in the top part of an enamel double boiler over low heat. Stir in the flour with a wooden spoon. Cook for a minute or two, stirring constantly, then add gradually 2 cups of the broth. Continue cooking a minute or two, add the chicken breasts, and keep warm over hot water until you are ready to serve. At that time stir in the cream, heat through, and place in a hot serving dish, sprinkle with parsley, and serve accompanied by flaky boiled rice and buttered fresh green peas cooked with white onions.

CHICKEN BRUNSWICK STEW
(SERVES 4)

2 *large plump whole chicken breasts (1½ pounds)*
4 *slices bacon, cut in small pieces*
2 *tablespoons butter*
1 *large yellow onion, peeled and sliced*
1 *No. 2 can (1-pound-3-ounce) tomatoes*
Salt and freshly ground pepper to taste
1 *bay leaf*
½ *teaspoon dried basil*
1 *can (15½-ounce) cut okra*
1 *package (10-ounce) frozen Fordhook lima beans*
1 *package (10-ounce) frozen sweet corn kernels*
4 *medium-sized new potatoes, peeled and sliced ¼ inch thick*
Dash of Tabasco
About 2 teaspoons Worcestershire sauce

Wash the chicken and dry on paper toweling. Place the bacon in a large casserole and heat over low fire until it is beginning to brown but is still limp. Add the butter, and when it is melted add the onion. Cook, stirring with a wooden spoon, until the onion is soft and lightly browned, or for about 5 minutes. Add the chicken breasts and cook 2½ minutes on each side. Add the tomatoes, and season well to taste with 1½ teaspoons salt and plenty of pepper. Add also the bay leaf and basil. Cover and cook gently, stirring occasionally, until the chicken is tender, or for about 45 minutes. Add the okra, including the juice, and continue cooking for about 15 minutes, stirring occasionally. Remove the chicken temporarily. Add the lima beans and corn and cook 15 minutes longer. In the meantime remove all skin and bones from the chicken, keeping the meat as whole as possible. Now add the potatoes and cook until tender, or for about 20 minutes longer. Bury the chicken in the juice and, when piping hot, season to taste with Tabasco and Worcestershire sauce. Serve at once on hot plates.

CHICKEN PIE, COUNTRY STYLE
(SERVES 6)

3 *whole chicken breasts*
About 5–6 cups water
12 *small white onions, peeled but left whole*
2 *large carrots, peeled and cut in 1-inch pieces*
1 *teaspoon salt*
6 *whole peppercorns*
3 *tablespoons butter*
3 *tablespoons flour*
Additional salt and pepper to taste

Wash the chicken, place in a pan, and cover with the water. Bring slowly to the boiling point, and skim carefully. Reduce the heat, add the onions, carrots, salt, and peppercorns. Simmer partially covered, skimming again if necessary, until the chicken is tender, or for about 1 hour. Cool until it may be handled, then remove and discard the skin and bones, leaving the chicken in large pieces. Place these in the bottom of a 2½- to 3-quart round baking dish, 3 inches deep. Add the carrots and onions. This should leave you about 2½ cups chicken broth.

Preheat the oven at this point to 475° and proceed to make the chicken gravy to be poured over the chicken. Melt the butter in a saucepan and add the flour. Stir with a wooden spoon over low heat for a minute or two, then add the strained chicken broth gradually and continue cooking until it is thickened, stirring constantly. Season to taste with a dash of pepper and more salt if necessary, and pour over the chicken. Now make biscuit dough as follows.

FOR THE BISCUITS

1 cup all-purpose flour sifted
2 teaspoons baking powder
¼ teaspoon salt
2 tablespoons soft butter
About ⅜ cup milk

Sift together the flour, baking powder, and salt. Add the butter and mix in thoroughly, using a large silver fork or pastry blender. Add enough milk to make a soft dough. Turn out on a floured pastry cloth or board, and toss lightly until the outside looks smooth. Roll out to ½-inch thickness and cut with a floured 2½-inch biscuit cutter, making at least 7 biscuits. Place these symmetrically over the chicken and gravy and place immediately in the hot oven. Bake until the biscuits are a golden brown, or for about 20 minutes. Serve at once.

BONED STUFFED CHICKEN BREASTS OLIVETTE
(SERVES 6–8)

Preheat oven to 425°

4 or 5 boned chicken breasts
1 pound fresh mushrooms
4 shallots, or 1 medium onion
¾ pound butter
Salt and coarsely ground black pepper
2½ tablespoons Hungarian paprika
Juice of 2 lemons
½ cup chopped parsley

Remove the skins from the chicken breasts. With a sharp knife slice in two lengthwise, being careful, however, not to cut all the way through. Wash, stem, peel, and slice fine the mushrooms. Peel the shallots and chop fine or substitute the equivalent amount of chopped onion. Cook the shallots a minute or two in ¼ pound of the butter, then add the mushrooms, and cook until the mushrooms have yielded their juice and boiled down and are just beginning to brown. Season lightly to taste with salt and pepper.

Stuff the chicken breasts with the mushrooms and place in a buttered baking dish large enough to hold them without crowding. Melt the remaining ½ pound butter and sprinkle it copiously with Hungarian paprika, about 2½ tablespoons, and plenty of salt and pepper, and then add the lemon juice and a lot of finely chopped parsley (at least ½ cup). Pour over the chicken. Place the dish in the preheated oven and bake, basting frequently, until the chicken is well done but not dried up—about 1 hour or slightly more.

ELEANOR'S CHICKEN-AND-NOODLES CASSEROLE
(SERVES 4–6)

Preheat oven to 375°

½ *pound wide egg noodles*

¼ *pound grated Parmesan and/or Romano cheese (generous measure)*

Salt and pepper

4 *cups cooked chicken meat*

4 *tablespoons butter*

4 *tablespoons flour*

2 *cups thin cream or whole milk*

2 *cups rich chicken stock*

Buttered crumbs (optional)

Boil the noodles until soft. Rinse in cold water. Drain. Reserve 2 tablespoons cheese and mix the rest with the noodles. Salt and pepper to taste. Arrange in a buttered baking dish and cover with the chicken. Melt the butter in a small pan, add the flour, and cook and stir until well blended. Heat the cream and stock and add to the butter and flour. Bring to a boil and pour over the chicken. Sprinkle with the remaining cheese and with buttered crumbs if desired. Bake in the preheated oven until thoroughly heated and browned.

COLD CHICKEN MOUSSE
(SERVES 6 TO 8)

2 *cups cooked chicken, cut in small pieces*
1 *cup clear cold chicken broth*
1 *small green pepper, washed, stemmed, seeds removed, coarsely cut*
3 *small white onions or shallots, peeled and sliced*
2 *stalks of the heart of celery, cut into ½-inch pieces*
Salt, freshly ground pepper, onion salt, Worcestershire sauce, Tabasco, paprika, to taste
1½ *tablespoons plain gelatin*
1 *cup heavy whipping cream*
1 *heart of Boston or Romaine lettuce, washed, dried, and chilled*
3 *tablespoons French dressing*
1 *ripe but firm avocado, peeled and sliced at the last moment*

Have ready all the ingredients listed above. Place the chicken in a blender along with 2 tablespoons of the cold chicken broth. Run the blender for a second or two. Add the green pepper and onions or shallots, and another 2 tablespoons cold broth, and run blender again for a second or two. Last of all add and blend the celery, using more broth if necessary to make a smooth mixture.

Place the mixture in a mixing bowl and season to taste with salt, pepper, onion salt, at least 1 tablespoon Worcestershire sauce, and a drop or two of Tabasco. Soak the gelatin for 20 minutes in ¼ cup cold water, then thoroughly dissolve it in ½ cup boiling-hot chicken broth. Stir in the dissolved gelatin. Whip the cream until stiff and fold it into the chicken mixture. Empty the mixture into a 2-quart round mold, rinsed first in cold water.

Refrigerate several hours, until it is firm to the touch. Run a spatula around the edge, and turn the mousse out onto a chilled shallow serving dish lined with the hearts of lettuce or Romaine. Trickle the French dressing over the greens, but not on the mousse. Garnish with the avocado, sprinkle the top of the mousse lightly with paprika, and serve.

CHICKEN SALAD
(SERVES 6–8)

Believe it or not, I had never concocted a chicken salad before making this one. I have, however, encountered various versions at New England church suppers.

2 3½-pound broiling chickens, cut up
2 or 3 small white onions, peeled
Several celery tops
2 quarts boiling water
1 tablespoon salt
2 heads Boston lettuce, outer leaves discarded, well washed, wrapped in a clean towel, and refrigerated until ready to use
2 cups Boiled Dressing (see page 49)
½ cup double-strength chicken broth, chilled until stiff
2 cups finely diced hearts of celery, minus threads
Chopped parsley, tarragon, or chives for decoration

Cook the chickens the day before you expect to make the salad: Wash them in cold water and place in a deep 4-quart pan; add the onions and celery tops. Pour over them the boiling water. Place over low heat and bring slowly to a boil, skim carefully, and simmer slowly until the chickens are tender, or about 1½ hours. Add the salt when half done. Remove from the heat and let the chickens cool in their own juice. Refrigerate until you are ready to proceed.

Remove the meat from the bones, discarding bones and skins. Strain the chicken broth back over the chicken and chill until you are ready to cut it into cubes. In the meantime make the Boiled Dressing (below). Also remove 1 cup of the jellied broth covering the cold chicken and boil until reduced to ½ cup; chill.

When you are ready to assemble the chicken salad, spread the lettuce over the bottom of a chilled shallow salad bowl or on plates. Beat the reduced jellied broth into the Boiled Dressing. Cube the chicken and add, along with the diced celery. Pile onto the lettuce leaves. Garnish with the chopped parsley, tarragon, or chives, and serve.

BOILED DRESSING
(2 GENEROUS CUPS)

1 *teaspoon salt*
2 *tablespoons sugar*
1 *tablespoon flour*
Dash of pepper
½ *cup cider vinegar*
¼ *cup water*
Yolks of 4 eggs
⅛ *pound butter* (4 *tablespoons*)
½ *to* 1 *cup thick cream or* 1 *cup sour cream*

Put in a small bowl the salt, sugar, flour, and pepper. Add, stirring until smooth, the vinegar and water. Beat the egg yolks well, add them to the mixture, then strain the whole into the top part of a small double boiler. Add the butter, place over boiling water, and cook, stirring furiously, until well thickened, but be careful to remove immediately from the fire the second the dressing is done so that it won't curdle. It should be quite thick, as it is to be thinned when cold with thick sweet cream or sour cream.

BAKED CHICKEN BREASTS
(SERVES 4)

Preheat oven to 375°

This recipe was contributed by a student at Haverford College who had heard that I was writing a New England cookbook and needed more chicken recipes. I tried it and am happy to include it, New England or not.

> 2 *whole chicken breasts, cut in two*
> *Salt to taste*
> 4 *tablespoons butter*
> ½ *cup grated Parmesan cheese*
> 4 *half strips of bacon*
> ¼ *cup Bacos (a General Mills soybean product)*
> 4 *tablespoons water or chicken broth for gravy*

Butter generously a pan large enough to hold the chicken breasts comfortably. Wash and dry the chicken breasts and place skin side up in the pan. Sprinkle lightly with salt and dot with butter. Sprinkle generously with grated Parmesan cheese. Place in the preheated oven and bake for 40 minutes, turning the chicken breasts over when golden brown, adding more butter and more cheese to the other side. Remove from the oven, turn the chicken breasts skin side up again, lay over each a half strip of bacon, and sprinkle with the Bacos. Continue baking for 20 minutes longer, basting with the drippings in the pan. Place the chicken breasts on a hot platter. Add water or broth to the pan and stir over low heat until the liquid is reduced to a small quantity of pan gravy. Pour over the chicken and serve at once, with mashed potatoes and one green vegetable.

BETSEY'S PARTY CHICKEN
(SERVES 6)

Preheat oven to 275°

> 12 *slices lean bacon, cut thin*
> 6 *half chicken breasts*
> 1 *can mushroom soup*
> ½ *pint sour cream*
> *Salt and pepper to taste*
> ½ *cup dry sherry* (*optional*)

Butter a baking dish thoroughly. Take 2 thin slices of bacon and wrap around each half chicken breast. Mix the mushroom soup and sour cream together. Salt and pepper to taste. Place some of this mixture in the bottom of the dish. Put in the chicken breasts and cover with the rest of the soup-and-sour-cream combination. Place in the preheated oven and bake for 3 hours. Skim off excess fat. Remove the cover and turn up the heat to 375° for the last 15 minutes to brown, and add sherry if you wish.

ELLEN'S FRIED-CHICKEN CASSEROLE
(SERVES 4)

Preheat oven to 350°

> ½ *cup plus 1 tablespoon flour*
> 2 *teaspoons salt*
> ½ *teaspoon pepper*
> 2 *whole chicken breasts, halved*
> 4–6 *tablespoons butter*
> 3–4 *tomatoes, peeled and sliced thick*
> ¼ *teaspoon tarragon*
> 1 *cup light cream*

Combine ½ cup of flour, the salt, and the pepper in a bag. Add the chicken breasts and shake. Keep the flour. Heat the butter and brown the chicken in it on all sides. Transfer to a casserole dish. Shake the tomato slices in the remains of the seasoned flour and sauté over medium heat until lightly browned. Arrange 4 or 5 slices of tomato around the chicken. Break up the remaining slices, sprinkle with tarragon, and place on top of the chicken. Add the remaining 1 tablespoon of flour to the skillet and stir to blend. Add the cream, stirring; simmer until thickened a bit. Pour the sauce over the chicken and tomatoes. Cover the casserole. Bake at 350° for 1 hour. Remove the cover for the last 15 minutes.

Note: For 2 people cook in foil pans and freeze half.

LUNCHEON DISH FOR ONE
(SERVES 1)
Preheat oven to 375°–400°
   2 *tablespoons soft butter*
   4 *half strips bacon, cooked until crisp*
   2 *slices white bread, crusts removed, but slices left whole*
   ¼ *cup heavy cream*
   2 *fresh eggs*
   Salt and pepper to taste

Butter a shallow 5½-inch shirred-egg dish with 1 teaspoon of the butter. Cook the bacon until almost crisp and keep warm. Toast the bread lightly on both sides and butter copiously with the remainder of the butter. Lay one of the slices butter side up in the dish and trickle over it 1 tablespoon of the cream. Cover with a second piece of toast, butter side up, and again trickle a tablespoon of the cream over the toast. Now break the two eggs carefully so as not to break the yolks, and slide them on top of the toast. Salt and pepper lightly to taste and pour the remainder of the cream over the eggs. Place the dish in the preheated oven and bake until the whites are opaque, or for about 10 minutes. Lay the strips of bacon over the eggs and eat at once.

BAKED EGGS IN TOMATOES
(SERVES 6)
Preheat oven to 375°–400°
            6 *large firm perfect tomatoes*
            Salt and pepper to taste

6 eggs
½ cup toasted bread crumbs
2 tablespoons butter

With a sharp knife cut off a slice from the stem end of each tomato. Scrape out the seeds, leaving as much of the pulp as possible. Salt and pepper lightly inside the tomato. Place side by side in a buttered baking dish just large enough to hold the tomatoes securely. Slip an egg out of its shell into each tomato. Sprinkle generously with the bread crumbs. Dot with butter. Place the dish in the preheated oven and bake until the whites of the eggs are set, or for about 25 to 30 minutes. Serve at once.

SCRAMBLED BREAKFAST EGGS WITHOUT THE SCRAMBLE
(SERVES 1–2)

2 eggs
½ cup milk
1 generous teaspoon butter
Salt and freshly ground pepper to taste

Break the eggs into a small bowl, and add the milk. Place the butter in the top part of a small, round-bottomed double boiler over a small quantity of boiling water. When the butter has melted, tilt the pan around to butter the sides. Beat the eggs and milk with a rotary beater 50 turns, pour into the pan, place over the boiling water, cover tightly, and cook 10 minutes without stirring. Run a knife around the edge and turn out the eggs, upside down, onto a hot plate. Sprinkle lightly with salt and pepper, and eat at once, accompanied by buttered toast.

RINKTUM DITTY
(SERVES 2)

2 *slices white toast*
3 *teaspoons butter*
½ *small onion, peeled and chopped fine*
2 *stewed tomatoes*
½ *teaspoon salt*
Pepper to taste
1 *teaspoon granulated sugar*
¼ *pound shredded American cheese*
1 *egg, slightly beaten*

Make 2 slices toast and butter each with 1 teaspoon of the butter. Keep hot. Melt the remaining teaspoon butter in a small heavy frying pan. Add the onion and cook until soft but not brown. Add the tomatoes, salt, pepper, and sugar, and simmer about 5 minutes. Add the cheese and cook over low heat, stirring constantly, until the cheese has melted. Now add the egg gradually, stirring constantly, and cook about 1 minute longer. Put the toast on 2 hot plates and cover with the hot mixture. Serve at once.

F O U R

Meats

HOME-CORNED BEEF

FUNDAMENTAL DIRECTIONS FOR CORNING BEEF
How to corn beef yourself. Personally I wouldn't bother, but
just for the fun of it I did try, and the results were good. By the
way, most New Englanders, for some reason, like to have the
kind of corned beef that is on the gray side, but I prefer
the pink variety.

Before proceeding with my testing of corned beef, I read in
Woman's Day Encyclopedia of Cooking, on page 485, this in-
formation:

TO CORN BEEF—This term covers a process by which protein
foods, meat, poultry, game and fish are preserved in a liquid
solution of salt, sugar and saltpeter, which is called brine. The
salt actually preserves the food, the sugar keeps the salt from
hardening the food, and the saltpeter intensifies and preserves the

color. After corning the food may be used as is, or processed further by smoking or drying.

Corning is a very old process of preserving meats. The term comes from the old English word "corn," meaning grain or any small particle, and it is a reminder that originally corning was done with dry granular salt, rather than in brine.

Foods to be corned should be fresh. Foods that have been frozen do not corn well since the cellular structure, already softened by the freezing, would be softened further to a mushy unpalatable taste by the corning process.

TO CORN MEAT (for a pink result)

Remove the bones and cut the meat into uniform pieces. For each 25 pounds of meat allow 3 pounds of granulated plain, not iodized, salt. Use a wooden or stone container. A layer of salt, a layer of meat, starting and ending with salt. Let stand overnight. Make a brine of 1 pound sugar, 1 tablespoon baking soda, 2 tablespoons saltpeter and 1 quart water. Pour the brine over the meat and weight the top to keep the meat under the brine. Keep in a cool place (under 45°). Cure for 4 to 6 weeks. Keep the meat in brine until ready to use.

Note: The cuts of beef most generally used for corning are rump, brisket, and plate.

NEW ENGLAND BOILED DINNER
(SERVES 6–8)

5 *pounds brisket of corned beef (the gray variety if you are very New England, the pink variety if you prefer it, as I do)*
6 *large carrots, peeled and cut in 2 crosswise*
6 *large parsnips, peeled and cut in 2 crosswise*
6–8 *small white turnips, peeled and left whole*
6–8 *small white onions, peeled*

1 *small green cabbage, about 1 pound, outer leaves removed, cut into 6–8 sections*

12 *small white potatoes, peeled*

6–8 *small beets (optional), well washed, with part of the leaves removed*

½ *pound lean salt pork, rinsed in cold water*

1 *tablespoon granulated sugar*

Pinch of soda

1 *tablespoon soft butter*

Parsley for garnishing

Wash the beef and soak it for 1 hour in cold water to cover. In the meantime, prepare all the vegetables, covering them temporarily with cold water. Wash the salt pork and place it in a large pot big enough to hold all the ingredients. Add the corned beef, and cover with plenty of cold water, probably 8 quarts. Bring very slowly to a simmer. It must not boil. Skim carefully for the first 10 minutes of simmering. Cover the pot, reduce the heat to the lowest possible point, and continue cooking until the meat is very tender, or for at least 4 or 5 hours. One hour before it will be done add the carrots, parsnips, and turnips, and the sugar. Half an hour later, start cooking the onions, cabbage, potatoes, and beets in separate pots, adding a pinch of soda to the cabbage.

Have ready a large heated platter, place the meat in the center of the dish, spread with soft butter, and quickly distribute all the vegetables, except the beets, around the meat. Remove the stems from the beets, pinch off the skins, and serve in a separate dish, so that they won't discolor the rest. Garnish the platter with parsley and send to the table to be carved and served on hot plates. Accompany with prepared mustard and Horseradish Sauce.

HORSERADISH SAUCE

1 *cup heavy cream*
2 *tablespoons white pickled horseradish*
2 *teaspoons prepared mustard*
½ *teaspoon salt*
¼ *teaspoon pepper*

Whip the cream until stiff. Mix together the well-drained horseradish, the mustard, salt, and pepper. Fold this into the whipped cream. Serve shortly after mixing.

RED FLANNEL HASH
(SERVES 4–6)

1 *generous cup finely chopped home-cooked corned beef left over from New England Boiled Dinner (see page 57)*
1 *cup chopped mixed vegetables left over from the same Boiled Dinner*
2 *cups coarsely chopped freshly boiled potatoes*
3 *or 4 small cooked beets, chopped fine (if necessary for color)*
6 *strips bacon*
About ¼ cup liquid from Boiled Dinner
2 *tablespoons soft butter*
1 *tablespoon chopped parsley*

Chop sufficient cold corned beef to make a generous cup of it. Add the same amount of mixed chopped vegetables left over from yesterday's Boiled Dinner. Peel and boil separately several potatoes, but do not overcook. Drain well and chop coarsely. Add to the other ingredients, along with the chopped beets. Cut the bacon in 1-inch squares, and cook them in a heavy iron or aluminum frying pan, over low heat, until crisp. Skim them out of the fat, and set aside to drain on paper toweling.

This should leave about ¼ inch of hot fat in the pan. Spread the hash smoothly to cover the bottom of the pan, and pour over it about ¼ cup liquid from the Boiled Dinner. Place the pan on very low heat and cook without stirring until the hash starts to brown around the edges, indicating that it has browned on the bottom. This will take half an hour or longer. Fold it like an omelet and turn out onto a hot platter. Dot with butter, sprinkle with crisp bacon and parsley, and serve on hot plates.

POT ROAST OF BEEF
(SERVES 4–6)

1 tablespoon flour
½ teaspoon salt
¼ teaspoon pepper
3 pounds shoulder roast of beef
1½ tablespoons lard
1 cup tomato juice
1 cup consommé
1 large yellow onion, peeled and chopped
2 whole cloves
1 bay leaf
4 large carrots, peeled and cut in 1-inch pieces
8 small white onions, peeled but left whole
3 large potatoes, peeled and quartered
1 tablespoon chopped parsley

Mix the flour with the salt and pepper, and dredge both sides of the roast with the mixture. Melt the lard in a heavy iron casserole, and when it is sizzling hot, place the meat in the pot and brown both sides. Heat together the tomato juice and consommé and pour over the meat, and add the chopped onion, cloves, and bay leaf. Cover and allow to simmer gently for about 2 hours, turning the meat over once. At this point add the carrots and the whole onions, and continue simmering for another hour, turning the meat over once more. Add the potatoes and cook until they are tender through, or for about 1 hour longer. Remove from the fire and allow to stand for 10 minutes or so, then skim off as much fat as possible. Reheat, sprinkle with parsley, and serve.

Note: This is even better reheated the next day in a 400° oven until the sauce thickens slightly, or for about 45 minutes.

BEEF STEW
(SERVES 4)

Preheat oven to 325°

2 *pounds boneless beef for stew, cut in 1½-inch cubes*

3 *tablespoons all-purpose flour*

3 *tablespoons bacon fat*

2 *medium-size onions, peeled and sliced fine*

1 *can (12-ounce) tomato juice*

1 *can (8-ounce) stewed tomatoes, preferably with onion and green pepper*

4 *large carrots, peeled and cut in rounds*

¾ *teaspoon salt*

Dash of freshly ground pepper

1 *heaping teaspoon granulated sugar*

1 *bay leaf*

24 *potato balls scooped out from large peeled potatoes*

Place the meat in a large plastic bag, add the flour and shake until the meat is lightly and evenly coated. Melt the bacon fat in a large (13-inch) heavy frying pan, and when sizzling hot add the onions and the meat, spreading it over the surface, and brown quickly and lightly all over. Transfer to an oven-proof casserole. Heat together the tomato juice and stewed tomatoes, place them in the frying pan, and stir with a wooden spoon to incorporate the brown residue in the pan. Pour this over the meat. Cover and place in a preheated oven to cook slowly until the meat is very tender, or for about 3 hours. After it has cooked 1 hour, add the carrots, salt, pepper, sugar, and bay leaf. In the meantime peel the large potatoes and with a scoop make the potato balls. Cover with cold water, and about ¼ hour before the stew will be done cook them in lightly salted water until just tender. Add them, well drained, to the stew, just before serving.

DRIED BEEF WITH EGGS
(SERVES 3)
1 *package (4 ounces) dried beef*
2 *cups boiling water*
4 *large eggs*
2 *tablespoons butter*
½ *cup heavy cream*
¼ *cup milk*

Pull the beef into smaller pieces. Place in a bowl and cover with boiling water. Allow to soak 2 minutes, drain, and pat dry on several thicknesses of paper toweling. Break the eggs into a small bowl. Melt the butter in a medium-size frying pan, add the beef, and stir with a wooden spoon. Add the cream gradually and stir over low heat for about 10 minutes. In the meantime beat the eggs with the milk until well mixed. Add to the beef and cream and stir constantly with a metal spoon until the eggs are almost but not quite set. Serve at once. Buttered green peas go well with this as a luncheon dish.

MEAT LOAF
(SERVES 6–8)

Preheat oven to 375°

1 ½ pounds ground top round ⎫ *This mixture can be found*
¾ pound ground veal   ⎬ *ready to use in certain*
¾ pound ground fresh pork ⎭ *good supermarkets*
4 slices white bread, crusts removed
1 ⅓ cups milk
3 whole eggs
2 tablespoons finely chopped celery
2 small onions, peeled and cut fine
2 tablespoons chopped parsley
2 teaspoons salt
Dash of freshly ground pepper
3 whole strips bacon
½ cup boiling water

Butter a large bread pan copiously. Place the three meats in a large bowl. Pluck the bread into small pieces and moisten with the milk. Break the 3 eggs onto the meat, add the celery, onions, parsley, and salt and pepper, and finally add the softened bread. With a large fork work the whole together until well mixed. Spread evenly and firmly in the buttered bread pan. Lay the strips of bacon over the top. Place in the preheated oven to bake for about 1½ hours or until brown on top and around the edges. When it has started to brown, or in about 45 minutes, pour over the meat the boiling water and continue cooking, basting occasionally with the juice which has formed. When done and ready to serve, pour off the juice, run a knife around the edge, and turn the loaf out onto a hot platter. Serve while hot with mashed potatoes and buttered, boiled celery.

SUSIE'S MEAT BALLS
(SERVES 4–6)

1 pound top sirloin, put through the grinder twice

½ cup quick-cooking oatmeal

1 egg, slightly beaten

1 teaspoon Worcestershire sauce

Salt and pepper to taste

1 tablespoon chopped parsley

2 shallots or small white onions, peeled and chopped fine

4 tablespoons butter

1 tablespoon flour

1 can consommé

4 tablespoons tomato ketchup

½ cup water

½ pound fresh mushrooms, washed and sliced fine

Extra chopped parsley for garnish

Mix together the first 6 ingredients and shape into 14 balls of equal size. Cook the shallots or onions in 2 tablespoons of the butter until lightly browned, sprinkle with the flour, stir well and gradually add the consommé. Thin the ketchup with the water and add to the sauce. Simmer 10 minutes. In the meantime prepare the mushrooms. Add these to the sauce, and simmer for ½ hour.

Brown the meat balls lightly on both sides in the remaining 2 tablespoons butter. Cover with the sauce and simmer for about

½ hour, adding a little more water if necessary. Garnish with parsley and serve.

SWEDISH MEAT BALLS
(SERVES 6–8)

Preheat oven to 350°
½ *cup soft bread crumbs*
1½ *cups milk*
½ *pound boneless tender beef* ⎱ *Both put through grinder*
½ *pound boneless lean pork* ⎰ *4 times*
1 *egg, slightly beaten*
1 *teaspoon salt*
Freshly ground pepper to taste
½ *teaspoon ground allspice*
1 *yellow onion, peeled and chopped fine*
2 *tablespoons bacon fat*
6 *tablespoons butter*
1 *teaspoon beef extract, dissolved in* 1½ *cups boiling water*
1½ *tablespoons flour*
1 *cup light cream*
1 *tablespoon chopped parsley*

Soak the bread crumbs in half the milk. When they are well moistened, add the meat and mix thoroughly. Stir in the egg, seasonings, and, gradually, the rest of the milk. Cook the onion in the bacon fat for about 5 minutes, but do not brown it. Chill the onion before stirring it into the meat mixture. Shape the mixture into balls with two soup spoons dipped in cold water.

Melt 2 tablespoons of the butter in an iron frying pan, add half the meat balls and fry, shaking the pan and turning the balls to brown evenly. Remove to an oven-proof pan with half the beef-extract broth and reserve the remainder for gravy. Place the browned meat balls in the oven. Repeat the process, using 2 more tablespoons butter and the rest of the meat-ball mixture. Add these to the first lot and return to the oven. Add the remainder of the broth to the frying pan, stir well, and add the broth to the first lot of meat gravy. Wash the frying pan, dry, and add the remaining 2 tablespoons butter. When it is melted, stir in the flour, cook for a minute or two, then add the reserved meat gravy, and when it is thickened, stir in the cream and pour over the meat balls. Sprinkle with parsley and serve piping hot.

Note: These may be cooked well ahead of time and reheated in the oven before serving.

VEAL STEW
(SERVES 6–8)

3 *pounds rump of veal cut in 1½-inch squares*
12 *cups cold water*
Bouquet of parsley, ½ bay leaf, 1 stalk celery with top
¼ *teaspoon thyme*
2 *whole cloves*
Salt to taste (about 1 teaspoon)
¼ *teaspoon ground pepper*
5 *carrots, peeled and cut in 1-inch pieces*
About 4 dozen little fresh pearl onions
Boiling water
½ *pound fresh mushrooms*
Juice of 1 lemon
12 *new potatoes, peeled but left whole*
1 *tablespoon chopped parsley*

Look the meat over carefully and cut out and discard any bits of white. Place it in a large enamel pan and cover with 6 cups of the cold water. Soak 1 hour, drain well, cover with the remaining 6 cups of cold water and bring slowly to a simmer, skimming carefully. Add the bouquet, thyme, and cloves, and cook gently for 1½ hours or until the meat is tender, adding salt to taste, about ½ teaspoon, and pepper.

In the meantime prepare the vegetables. Peel and cut the carrots, cover with cold water, add ½ teaspoon salt, and cook until tender and almost all the water has boiled away. Set aside.

To peel and cook the onions, pour boiling water over them and let stand 3 minutes. Remove and place in cold water. Cut off the root end and gently squeeze toward the stem end. The onions will slip out unblemished. Make 2 small gashes in each root end with the tip of a paring knife. Cook in boiling water 5 minutes. Drain, cover with more boiling water, and cook until just tender, or for about 10 minutes. Drain partially and set aside. Remove the tough ends of the mushrooms, wash if necessary, peel, and quarter. Cover them temporarily with cold water to which you have added the lemon juice.

Peel the potatoes but leave them whole; cover with cold water and set aside. Chop the parsley.

About 15 minutes before the meat will be done, add the drained mushrooms to the meat and continue cooking. Put the potatoes on to cook in lightly salted water until tender through (about 15 minutes).

FOR THE SAUCE

> *4 tablespoons butter*
> *4 tablespoons flour*
> *Strained juice of 1 lemon*
> *3 egg yolks*
> *¾ cup heavy cream*
> *Pinch of nutmeg*

Drain off most of the broth from the stew, and strain through a fine sieve. Melt the butter in a 2-quart pan and stir in the flour, cooking without browning for a minute or two, then gradually add the broth. When smooth and thick add the lemon juice and any remaining juice on the meat. Place the pan over boiling water and gradually stir in the egg yolks and cream beaten together with a pinch of nutmeg. Cook for a minute or two.

Now add the onions and the carrots with their juice to the meat. Bring just to the boiling point and stir in the sauce. Do not allow to boil, once the sauce is added. Remove from the fire, drain the potatoes, and place them on top of the stew. Place all in a serving dish. Sprinkle with chopped parsley and serve on hot plates.

BAKED VEAL CUTLETS IN SOUR CREAM
(SERVES 4)

Preheat oven to 350°

1 *large green pepper, washed, split in two lengthwise, seeds removed*

3 *small white onions, peeled*

2 *tablespoons butter*

1 *pound veal cutlet cut about ½ inch thick*

3 *tablespoons water*

Salt and pepper to taste

½ *pint pasteurized homogenized sour cream*

½ *cup sweet heavy cream*

Paprika

Parboil together the green pepper and onions for 10 minutes in lightly salted water to cover. Wipe the meat dry on paper toweling. Melt the butter in a heavy frying pan, and when it is sizzling hot, add the veal. Cook until lightly browned on both sides, turning pieces over once or twice. Transfer to a round baking dish about 7 inches wide and 2½ inches deep. Add the 3 table-spoons water to the brown residue in the frying pan and stir over low heat with a wooden spoon until syrupy. Pour over the meat. Sprinkle with salt and pepper to taste. Drain the vegetables and cut the pepper in strips 1 inch wide and lay over the meat, then add the onions coarsely chopped. Soften the sour cream with the sweet cream and spread over all. Bake in the preheated oven for about 1 hour. Sprinkle lightly with paprika before serving.

VEAL POT PIE
(SERVES 4–6)

FOR THE BROTH

2¾-*pound roast of veal, cut from the leg, with bone included*
3 *quarts cold water*
1 *small white turnip, peeled*
2 *medium-size onions, peeled*
3 *carrots, peeled*
1 *bunch celery leaves*
1 *tablespoon salt*
3 *whole peppercorns*

First make the broth. Cut the meat away from the bone, in mouth-size pieces, discarding any white membrane or gristle encountered. Refrigerate until you are ready to make the stew. Place the veal bone in a large enamel pot and cover with the 3 quarts cold water. Allow to stand for half an hour. Bring slowly to a boil and skim carefully. Add the vegetables, salt, and pep-percorns. Simmer for about 3 hours, skimming if necessary.

Strain through a fine sieve, cool, and refrigerate until you are ready to use it.

FOR THE STEW

Meat from the roast, cut in 1-inch squares

4 tablespoons all-purpose flour

1 teaspoon salt

Dash of pepper

6–8 tablespoons butter

2 cups veal broth

2 small onions, peeled and chopped fine

6 carrots, peeled and cut in small pieces

Wipe the cubes of veal clean on paper toweling and dredge with the flour seasoned with the salt and pepper. Melt the butter and sauté the meat until well browned. Add the veal broth, stirring with a wooden spoon to make a smooth gravy. Simmer covered for about 1½ hours or until the veal is tender. Add the onions and carrots half an hour before the stew will be done. Place in an oven-proof casserole.

FOR THE BISCUIT TOPPING

Preheat oven to 450°–475°

2 cups all-purpose flour, sifted

½ teaspoon salt

½ teaspoon baking soda

1 teaspoon cream of tartar

4 tablespoons fresh lard

1 cup milk (about)

Sift together the flour, salt, soda, and cream of tartar. Work the lard into this with your fingertips and moisten with the milk. Turn out on a well-floured board or cloth and knead lightly until smooth. Roll out to ½-inch thickness and cut with a small biscuit cutter. Cover the top of the still-hot stew with the biscuits, place in the preheated oven, and bake until the biscuits are lightly browned, or for about 25 minutes. Serve immediately.

SAUTÉED VEAL KIDNEYS
(SERVES 4–6)

4 veal kidneys
Salt and freshly ground pepper to taste
6 tablespoons butter
Strained juice of 1 lemon
1 tablespoon chopped parsley

To prepare the kidneys, wash in cold water, and remove the thin membrane. Slice crosswise into pieces ¼ inch thick. Cut again into smaller pieces, discarding the white central fat and sinew. Soak in cold water ½ hour. Rinse again in cold water and pat thoroughly dry on paper toweling. Sprinkle with salt and pepper. Melt 4 tablespoons butter in a heavy medium-size frying pan. When sizzling hot, add the kidneys and sauté quickly, stirring with a wooden spoon, for not more than 5 minutes. Add the remaining 2 tablespoons butter and sprinkle with the lemon juice. Place in a hot serving dish, garnish with chopped parsley, and serve accompanied by Onions Baked in Milk (see p. 100).

BROILED LAMB KIDNEYS
(SERVES 4)

10 large fresh lamb kidneys
Milk
Salt, paprika, celery seed, marjoram, and onion powder to taste
2 tablespoons fresh lemon juice
¼ pound butter

The night before you expect to serve the kidneys, soak them overnight in cold water to cover, placing them in the refrigerator. Drain them well the next morning, rinse them off in cold water, place them back in the dish, cover them with milk, and refrigerate again until you are ready to cook them.

Preheat your broiler. Line the broiling pan with heavy-duty foil. Drain the milk from the kidneys, rinse them in cold water, and with a sharp knife split them in two lengthwise, making moon-shaped pieces. With sharp little scissors carefully cut out and discard the white tough parts. Spread the kidneys out on the broiling pan with cut side up, and sprinkle to taste with the seasonings. Dot generously with the butter.

Place under the broiling unit, far enough away so that the kidneys will cook slowly, and broil about 8 minutes. Turn over onto the other side and sprinkle generously with the lemon juice. Continue broiling for about 8 minutes longer. Baste with their own buttery juice. Transfer to a hot platter and serve at once, accompanied by a purée of fresh carrots.

BOILED LAMB CHOPS WITH CAPER SAUCE
(SERVES 6)

6 *double loin lamb chops*
1½ *quarts hot water, about*
6 *large carrots, peeled and halved*
8 *small white onions*
1 *teaspoon salt*
6 *small purple-top white turnips, peeled and left whole*
6 *small white potatoes*
8 *tablespoons butter*
8 *tablespoons all-purpose flour*
4 *cups broth from the lamb*

1 small (3¼-ounce) bottle capers in vinegar
Dash of pepper
1 tablespoon chopped parsley

Cut away and discard most of the fat from the chops. Place in a heavy pot and cover with the hot water. Bring slowly to a simmer. Skim carefully. Add the carrots and 2 of the onions. When the liquid comes to a simmer again, skim, cover partially, and cook for 1 hour and 15 minutes. Add the salt, the remaining 6 onions, and the turnips. Continue cooking 15 minutes; add the potatoes and cook until they are tender through, for almost half an hour longer.

Remove from the fire temporarily and strain off the broth. This should give you about 4 cups. In the top part of a double boiler, melt the butter, add the flour, and stir with a wooden spoon over low flame for about 2 minutes without browning, then add gradually about 4 cups of the broth, making a smooth, fairly thick sauce. Drain the capers, saving the juice. Add the capers to the sauce and part of the juice, to taste. Pour the sauce back over the meat and vegetables, add a dash of pepper, heat thoroughly, and place in a hot serving dish. Sprinkle with parsley and serve.

LAMB CASSEROLE
(SERVES 6)

½ leg of lamb (about 4 pounds)
4 tablespoons butter
Dash of freshly ground pepper
½ teaspoon salt
4 tablespoons flour
3 cups boiling water

1 *cup dry white wine*

A *bouquet of 1 sprig parsley, ½ teaspoon thyme, 1 bay leaf, 1 small clove garlic*

1 *can (6-ounce) tomato purée*

1 *can (3-ounce) whole mushroom crowns*

2 *large carrots (peeled and sliced)*

6 *white onions (about ¼ pound), peeled and left whole*

1 *leek (white part only), washed, split lengthwise, and cut crosswise*

1 *medium-sized purple-top turnip, peeled and cut into 6 pieces*

6 *new potatoes, peeled and cut in 2*

1 *package frozen peas*

2 *tablespoons finely chopped parsley for garnish*

Trim off all fat and dried skin from the roast. Brown slowly in butter, in an electric or iron skillet. When the meat is lightly browned all over, remove temporarily. Add pepper and salt to the flour and sprinkle into the remaining butter in the casserole. Stir well with a wooden spoon, and when the mixture is free from lumps, add gradually 1 cup of the boiling water and the wine. Also add the bouquet and the tomato purée. Stir until smooth and replace the meat. Cover and simmer very gently for about 2 hours, turning the meat over occasionally.

At this point add the mushrooms and their juice, the sliced carrots, the onions, leek, and turnip, and continue cooking for another hour, turning the meat over as before. Now add the potatoes and cook until they are tender through, or for about ½ hour longer. Remove from the heat and cool partially.

When cool enough to handle, remove the meat to a platter and cut the meat into bite-size pieces, discarding any bone or gristle encountered. Before returning the meat to the sauce, carefully skim off any excess fat. Discard the bouquet. Empty the whole into a pretty serving casserole. Cover and reheat in a 350° oven until sizzling hot.

In the meantime cook the peas, following directions on the package. Drain thoroughly and place them in a mound in the center of the casserole. Sprinkle with chopped parsley and serve with crisp Portuguese or French bread to mop up the gravy.

MADAME BRISSAUD'S POACHED LEG OF LAMB WITH SAUCE BÉARNAISE
(SERVES 8)

Obviously, this is not a New England recipe, but I served it so often while living in Little Compton that I am including it.

FOR THE LAMB

> *6–7-pound leg of lamb*
> *Large pot of boiling water*
> *12 juniper berries*
> *½ cup white pepper*
> *1 tablespoon salt*
> *10 cloves garlic*
> *Fresh parsley*

First, boil a large square of linen and hang it up to dry. In the meantime, with a sharp knife remove every vestige of outer skin and fat from the leg of lamb. Fill a large pot with water, big enough to hold the leg of lamb with the water comfortably, and heat to the boiling point. Add the juniper berries, pepper, salt, and garlic. Now wrap the lamb neatly in the square of linen, and sew it up securely, using a large needle and strong white thread. Place the lamb in the pot of hot, seasoned water. Watch carefully until it comes to the boiling point, then reduce the heat and allow the lamb to simmer very gently, allowing 15 minutes

for every pound of lamb (after trimming) and not one minute
longer. When cooked, remove the lamb from the water, cut
away the linen, place the lamb on a hot platter, garnish with
fresh parsley, and send to the table to be carved and served on
hot plates, accompanied by a large bowl of peeled, boiled new
potatoes and Béarnaise Sauce.

Note: The lamb should be a pale pink when served.

FOR THE BÉARNAISE SAUCE

> 1¾ cups tarragon vinegar
> 6 shallots, peeled and chopped fine
> 10 freshly crushed black peppercorns
> ½ teaspoon salt
> 8 slightly beaten egg yolks
> ½ cup soft butter
> 2 cups melted butter
> 3 branches fresh tarragon, chopped

Put the vinegar, shallots, crushed peppercorns, and salt into the
top part of an enamel double boiler and boil until but ½ cup is
left. Remove from the fire, and when the mixture is cold, add the
egg yolks and the soft butter. Set the pan in hot water (but not
boiling) and stir furiously with a wire whisk until the mixture
is thick. Remove from the fire and pass through a fine sieve. Put
the mixture back into a double boiler, but off the fire, and add,
little by little, the melted butter. If by any chance this should
curdle, add a lump of ice, stir furiously, and add another egg
yolk. Just before serving, stir in the chopped tarragon. Don't
try to serve this sauce too hot—it just can't be done, as heat
enough to make it hot curdles it. It must be made at the last
minute, however.

SHEPHERD'S PIE
(SERVES 4)

Preheat oven to 450°

FOR THE MEAT

    4 cups cold roast lamb put through a meat grinder
    ½ cup or more clear leftover lamb gravy
    ¾ cup canned beef broth or consommé
    2 tablespoons butter
    1 tablespoon flour
    1 teaspoon Worcestershire sauce
    Salt and freshly ground pepper to taste
    1 cup finely diced boiled carrots

Prepare the meat and place in a lightly buttered 1½-quart oval baking dish. Heat together the clear lamb gravy and the canned beef broth. Melt the butter in a small pan and stir in the flour. Cook a minute or two, stirring with a wooden spoon, and gradually add the hot broth and gravy, making a smooth sauce. Season to taste with about 1 teaspoon Worcestershire sauce and a slight amount of salt and pepper. Pour over the meat and stir in the drained cooked carrots. Set aside while you make the mashed potatoes.

FOR THE MASHED-POTATO TOPPING

    1½ pounds white potatoes, peeled and quartered
    1 teaspoon salt
    3 tablespoons butter
    About ¼ cup hot milk

Cover the potatoes with water, add the salt, bring to a boil, and cook until tender. Drain well. Add 2 tablespoons of the butter, mash well, and gradually add the hot milk.

When the potatoes are light and fluffy, spread evenly over the meat. Dot with the remaining tablespoon butter and bake until the pie is sizzling hot and the potatoes are a golden brown, or for about 30 to 40 minutes. Serve immediately.

OVEN-BARBECUED SPARERIBS
(SERVES 4)

1½ *pounds spareribs*
½ *small onion, chopped fine*
1 *tablespoon butter*
1 *tablespoon vinegar*
1 *tablespoon dark-brown sugar*
2 *tablespoons lemon juice*
½ *cup ketchup*
1½ *tablespoons Worcestershire sauce*
1 *teaspoon prepared mustard*
½ *cup water*
¼ *cup chopped parsley*
½ *teaspoon salt*
¼ *teaspoon coarsely ground pepper*
Extra chopped parsley

Place the ribs on a rack in a small roasting pan and allow them to stay at room temperature while you make the barbecue sauce. Cook the onion in the butter on a low flame until it is transparent but not brown. Add the vinegar, sugar, lemon juice, ketchup, Worcestershire sauce, prepared mustard, water, parsley, salt, and pepper. Simmer for about 20 minutes, stirring occasionally.

In the meantime preheat the oven to 450°. Place the ribs in the oven and bake for about 45 minutes, at which time pour off all the fat, removing the rack, and put the roast down into the pan. Pour half the sauce over the ribs, reduce the heat of the oven to 300°, and continue cooking for about 30 minutes. Turn the meat over and pour the remainder of the sauce over the second side and continue cooking for another hour, basting occasionally and adding, if necessary, a very little hot water to keep the sauce from burning. Transfer to a small hot meat platter, sauce and all. Sprinkle with extra chopped parsley, cut into four servings, and send to the table at once, accompanied by a Purée of Rutabagas and Potatoes (see page 93).

BAKED PORK CHOPS IN SOUR CREAM
(SERVES 4)

Preheat oven to 350°

> 4 *center-cut loin pork chops*
> 2 *small white onions*
> 1 *large green pepper*
> ½ *pint pasteurized homogenized sour cream*
> ½ *cup sweet heavy cream*
> 1 *tablespoon butter*
> ¼ *cup water*
> *Salt and freshly ground pepper to taste*
> 1 *tablespoon chopped parsley*

Wipe the chops clean with paper toweling. Peel the onions and split the pepper lengthwise. Remove and discard the stem and seeds. Parboil the pepper and onion together in salted water to cover, for 10 minutes. Soften the sour cream with the sweet cream. Melt the butter in a heavy frying pan over moderate heat. Add the chops and brown slowly on both sides, turning them over two or three times. Place the browned chops in a shallow oven-proof rectangular dish about 10 inches by 6 inches by 2 inches deep.

Pour off the excess fat in the frying pan, and add the ¼ cup water. Bring to a boil, stirring with a wooden spoon, and cook for a minute or two until syrupy. Pour this over the chops, and sprinkle with salt and pepper to taste. Drain the vegetables and cut the pepper in 1-inch strips lengthwise. Lay these over the meat. Slice the onions and lay on the peppers. Cover the whole with the softened sour cream. Place in the preheated oven and bake slowly for about 1 hour and 15 minutes. Sprinkle with parsley and serve accompanied by fluffy mashed potatoes.

BROILED PORK CHOPS WITH VEGETABLES
(SERVES 4–6)

Preheat oven to 475°

6 *thick center-cut pork chops*

2 *tablespoons flour*

Salt and pepper to taste

4 *medium-sized tomatoes, washed and cut in two crosswise*

1 *cup dried bread crumbs*

6 *small sweet potatoes, peeled after parboiling*

1 *16-ounce can green peas, well drained*

3 *tablespoons butter*

1 *tablespoon chopped parsley*

Dust the chops on both sides with the flour seasoned with a little salt and pepper. Spread the chops over the grill part of a broiler pan. Butter the broiler pan itself and arrange the tomatoes in a row down the center. Sprinkle them generously with the bread crumbs. Put the sweet potatoes down the two sides of the pan, and place the peas between the tomatoes and the sweet potatoes.

Sprinkle lightly with salt and a very little pepper. Dot the tomatoes with the butter. Place the rack with the chops over the
vegetables. Broil for 15 minutes, not too close to the broiling
unit, and turn the chops over and continue broiling for about
15 minutes longer. If there is any doubt in your mind that the
chops are quite done, slip the pan into the oven for 5 or 10 minutes longer. When ready to serve, lift the rack away from the
vegetables and tuck the chops here and there. Sprinkle with
parsley and serve.

PORK-CHOP SWEET-POTATO CASSEROLE
(SERVES 2)

Preheat oven to 350°

        4 small sweet potatoes (about ¾ pound)
        1 tablespoon butter
        ¾ teaspoon salt
        Dash of coarsely ground black pepper
        1 large Winesap apple
        2 medium-size white onions (optional)
        1 tablespoon light-brown sugar
        Juice and grated rind of 1 lemon
        1 tablespoon hot water
        2 thick loin pork chops (about 1 pound)

Butter a 1-quart baking dish. Wash and peel the sweet potatoes.
Slice crosswise into pieces ¼-inch thick and place in the dish.
Dot with the butter and sprinkle with the salt and pepper. Peel,
quarter, and core the apples, peel the onions, and slice both over
the sweet potatoes. Combine the brown sugar with the lemon
rind and juice, and spread over the apples. Add the hot water
and cover with the pork chops, from which you have trimmed

off part of the fat. Cover the dish and bake in the preheated oven until the chops are very tender, or for about 1½ hours. Remove the cover the last 30 minutes to brown the chops.

LUMBERJACK PIES
(MAKES 5 EIGHT-INCH PIES; SERVES 16 TO 20)

FOR THE FILLING

Plenty of parsley
12 whole cloves
½ teaspoon basil
½ teaspoon orégano
½ teaspoon rosemary
1½ teaspoons powdered sage
1½ teaspoons powdered cinnamon
3 pounds fresh pork shoulder
3 pounds chuck beef
3 quarts cold water
2 tablespoons salt
½ teaspoon coarsely ground pepper
3 or 4 large outer stalks of celery, washed, threads removed
1 large Bermuda onion, peeled, cut in half
2 pounds potatoes, peeled, washed, and quartered
2 tablespoons butter
Large jar of tart green relish

First make a bouquet garni of the parsley, cloves, basil, orégano, rosemary, and sage, tying securely in a piece of cheesecloth. Wash the two roasts quickly in cold water, sprinkle with cinnamon, and place them in a deep pot large enough to hold them comfortably. Cover with the 3 quarts cold water. Bring slowly to the simmering point (which will take at least 30 minutes), at which time skim carefully and add the salt and pepper, the bouquet garni, the celery, and the Bermuda onion, and cover the pan. Simmer gently for about 5 hours, until the meat falls from the bones. Strain, carefully reserving the stock. When they are cool enough to handle, save the onion and celery, discard the bouquet, and pull the meat from the bones, discarding all the fat and gristle. Run the meat through the grinder, along with the celery and onion, using the coarsest knife.

Meanwhile, boil the potatoes until tender, in lightly salted water. Drain and mash with the butter. Add the potatoes to the meat and mix well, adding sufficient reserved stock to make the mixture the consistency of mincemeat, or about 2½ cups. When cold, place in quart freezing containers and store in the freezer until needed; freeze any remaining broth separately. When ready to make a pie, defrost one container of the filling, and about ½ cup of the broth and mix the two.

Preheat oven to 350°

FOR THE CRUSTS

   2 *packages frozen unbaked pie crusts in aluminum pie pans*

Follow the directions on the package of frozen crusts, taking two from the package. Put the meat-and-potato filling into the bottom crust, loosening the edge of the crust from the pan. Loosen the edge of the slightly thawed second crust, and lift it from the pan, placing it over the filling. Tuck the top edge under the bottom. Seal the edges well. Crimp the edge. Cut several slits in the top. Bake on a cookie sheet, near the center of the oven, for 45 to 50 minutes or until the crust is lightly browned all over.

SALT PORK AND MILK GRAVY
(SERVES 4)
This traditional Vermont dish sounds awful, but is heavenly.

> ¾ *pound fresh fat salt pork*
> ¼ *cup pork drippings or bacon fat*
> ¼ *cup flour and more*
> 2 *cups milk (scalding hot)*
> ½ *teaspoon salt or salt to taste*

Be fussy about the salt pork you buy. The fat should be white and the lean pink. Cut away the outer edge or rind if any, then slice the pork evenly in pieces ¼ inch thick. Cover these with cold water and bring gently to a boil to remove excess salt. Drain well and dry the pieces on paper toweling. Melt the pork drippings or bacon fat in an iron frying pan (spider, so-called). Roll the pieces of salt pork in plenty of flour, and when the fat has melted, add them to the frying pan. Cook gently until well browned on both sides, turning the pieces over and over, for about 20 minutes. Remove to a hot serving dish and keep warm while you make the gravy.

Pour off all but about 4 tablespoons of the fat in the frying pan, and add to the remaining drippings the ¼ cup flour. Stir well with a wooden spoon until the paste is lightly brown, then gradually add the hot milk, making a smooth gravy. Season to taste with salt. Pour over the crisp warm pieces of pork and serve at once.

BAKED HAM
(SERVES 6)

Preheat oven to 325°

> ½ precooked ham (about 7 pounds)
> About 2 dozen whole cloves
> ½ cup maple syrup
> 1½ cups water
> ½ cup dry bread crumbs
> 2 tablespoons light-brown sugar
> ¼ teaspoon cinnamon

With a sharp knife carefully cut away the brown part of the fat. Score the fat in a diamond pattern and stick a whole clove down into each diamond. Place the ham in a small roasting pan. Mix the maple syrup and water together and pour over the ham. Place in the preheated oven and bake for about 1½ hours, basting every 15 minutes with the syrupy juice in the bottom of the pan. Add a little more water if necessary to prevent the syrup from thickening too much. Remove the ham from the oven temporarily and sprinkle the top with the bread crumbs mixed with the sugar and cinnamon, patting them on evenly. Return to the oven and bake 25 to 30 minutes longer or until the crumbs begin to brown, basting once or twice with the juice in the bottom of the pan. Transfer to a hot platter and skim off any clear fat from the crumby mixture in the roasting pan, then pour it around the ham. Serve sliced very thin with a sharp knife.

FIVE

Vegetables

ASPARAGUS IN CUSTARD
(SERVES 4–6)

Preheat oven to 325°–350°

3 *cups cooked tender green asparagus, cut in 2-inch pieces*
Salt and pepper to taste
½ *teaspoon dill salt or dill weed (crumbled)*
6 *eggs*
3 *cups milk*
1 *cup Buttered Croutons (page 9)*

Place the asparagus, well drained, in a 1-quart oven-proof dish. Sprinkle with the salt, pepper, and dill salt or dill weed. Beat the eggs, add the milk, and pour over the asparagus. Place the dish in a pan of hot water in the preheated oven and bake until the custard is set in the center, or for about 40 to 45 minutes. Serve with a few hot Buttered Croutons as a garnish.

JON STROUPE'S ASPARAGUS TART
(SERVES 6)

Preheat oven to 450°

FOR THE FILLING

4 cups tender, fresh asparagus, cut in ¼-inch pieces
2 tablespoons butter
3 tablespoons flour
¾ cup rich milk or cream
Salt and white pepper to taste
Dash of freshly grated nutmeg

Prepare the asparagus and cook in lightly salted boiling water until just tender, about 6 to 8 minutes. Drain and keep warm. Now make a cream sauce, using the butter, flour, and milk or cream, and season to taste with salt, pepper, and nutmeg. Add the cooked asparagus. Keep warm.

FOR THE PASTRY

1 cup flour
¼ teaspoon salt
⅓ cup lard
2 or 3 tablespoons ice water

Now mix and bake the tart shell. Sift together the flour and salt and work in the lard with your fingertips. Add enough ice water to make a dough that holds together. Shape into a ball and roll out into a circle large enough to line a 9-inch tart pan. Prick with a fork and bake until lightly browned in the preheated oven.

Fill with the creamed asparagus. Reduce the heat of the oven to 400° and bake the filled tart just long enough to heat through or until lightly browned, about 10 minutes. Serve at once, cut into 6 equal pieces.

POKE STALKS

These look vaguely like very young asparagus when they first poke their heads above ground, early in the spring. This is the time to gather them. I've seen them many times in Little Compton, but never mustered enough courage to gather them. Recently I encountered them for sale at the farmers' market in Wayne, Pennsylvania, and timidly bought a bunch, which I ate all alone in bed. They were certainly first cousins to asparagus, and this is how I cooked them, following directions given in an old cookbook dated 1871.

First I washed them well in cold water, but did not cut off the leaves at the tops. I then scraped the stems and laid them in cold salted water and let them soak for 2 hours. I tied them in a little bundle, using white string, as I do asparagus, then dropped them into a saucepan of boiling water and cooked them about 45 minutes. When they were done, the string was removed and the poke was laid tenderly on a piece of well-buttered toast, and a little extra melted butter was dribbled over all. Very good indeed!

DELECTABLE CARROTS
(SERVES 4)

5 *medium carrots*
1½ *cups lightly salted boiling water*
1 *teaspoon cornstarch*
1 *tablespoon granulated sugar*

¼ *teaspoon salt*
¼ *teaspoon powdered ginger*
⅓ *cup freshly squeezed, strained orange juice*
2 *tablespoons butter*

Wash and peel the carrots and slice thin, crosswise. Cook, covered, in the lightly salted boiling water until just tender, or for about 20 minutes. Watch carefully toward the last, as by the time they are done there may be no water left. Drain if necessary. Set aside. Mix together in a small saucepan the cornstarch, sugar, salt, and ginger, and moisten with the orange juice. Stir until smooth, and cook, stirring constantly, until the mixture thickens and bubbles, then cook 1 minute. Stir in the butter, pour over the carrots, and toss to coat evenly. Serve piping hot.

BAKED ACORN SQUASH
(SERVES 6)

Preheat oven to 350°

3 *large acorn squash*
6 *teaspoons butter*
2 *teaspoons grated orange rind*
2 *teaspoons grated lemon rind*
Salt and freshly ground pepper to taste
2 *tablespoons strained lemon juice*
2 *tablespoons strained orange juice*
2 *tablespoons dry or sweet sherry (optional)*

Butter copiously a cake tin large enough to hold 6 squash halves comfortably. Wash the squash and split in two with a sturdy knife. Remove the seeds and strings. Place the cut sides down on the tin. Bake in the preheated oven until tender (about 45 minutes). Cut a small piece off each curved side so that the squash will stand even when turned hollow side up. Place a teaspoon of butter in each hollow. Divide the grated orange and lemon peel evenly, adding it to the butter, sprinkle with salt and a little pepper, moisten with the strained juices and the sherry, and continue baking—about 15 minutes longer—basting once with the juice.

BAKED WINTER BUTTERNUT SQUASH
(SERVES 4)

Preheat oven to 375°

> *1 pound winter squash*
> *4 tablespoons butter*
> *½ cup light-brown sugar*
> *½ teaspoon salt*
> *Dash of pepper*
> *¼ cup cold water*
> *Few drops of fresh lemon juice (optional)*

Wash the squash, split lengthwise in two, discard the seeds, and peel. Cut in ¾-inch cubes. Rinse again. Place in a baking dish in layers, dotting each with the butter and sprinkling with the sugar. Sprinkle with salt and pepper and over all pour the cold water. Bake for about 1 hour, or until the squash is tender through. Stir gently once or twice as it cooks. A few drops of lemon juice may be sprinkled over all, just before serving, but this is optional.

SWEET-POTATO-AND-APPLE CASSEROLE
(SERVES 4)

Preheat oven to 400°

   1 pound (4 medium-sized) sweet potatoes (not yams)
   3 large McIntosh apples
   4 tablespoons butter, and more
   ½ cup light-brown sugar

Butter a quart baking dish. Parboil the well-washed sweet potatoes for about 25 minutes. Peel the apples, quarter, and core
them, then cut once more, making 8 slices of each apple. Peel
the sweet potatoes as soon as they are cool enough to handle, and
slice crosswise, in pieces almost 1 inch thick. Arrange the potatoes and apples in alternate layers in the baking dish, dotting
with the butter and sprinkling with the sugar. Cover the dish,
place in the preheated oven, and bake for about 35 to 40 minutes, basting once or twice with the syrup formed. Serve with
roast chicken or pork chops.

SWEET-POTATO PIE
(SERVES 6)

Preheat oven to 400°

       Pastry for a 1-crust pie (see page 169)
       1½ pounds sweet potatoes
       ¼ pound sweet butter, melted
       ⅔ cup superfine sugar
       3 eggs, slightly beaten
       1½ tablespoons brandy
       1 tablespoon rose water

½ *teaspoon grated nutmeg*
1½ *teaspoons cinnamon*
Pinch of salt

Line a 9-inch pie plate with plain pastry and crimp the edges. Refrigerate while you make the filling. Wash and peel the potatoes, cut in quarters, cover with water, and cook until tender, or for about 20 minutes. Drain and mash. Stir in the butter and sugar. Add the eggs, brandy, rose water, spices, and salt. Rub through a sieve and place in the pastry-lined plate. Bake in the preheated oven until the filling tests done in the center, or for about 35 to 40 minutes.

SCOOTIN'-'LONG-THE-SHORE
(SERVES 4)

This dish, which has long been popular on Cape Cod, Martha's Vineyard, and Nantucket, derives its name from its preparation by fishermen while at their work.

¼ *cup bacon fat*
1 *cup thinly sliced white onions*
2 *large potatoes, washed, peeled, and sliced thin*
Salt and freshly ground pepper to taste

Melt the bacon fat in a heavy skillet, and when it is sizzling hot, add the onions and stir them around with a wooden spoon. Add the potatoes and cook over low heat for a few minutes; sprinkle lightly with salt and pepper. Cover tightly and continue cooking, stirring occasionally, until the potatoes are soft, or for about 25 minutes. Remove the cover and continue cooking without stirring until the mixture is crispy on the bottom. Turn out onto a hot platter and serve at once.

PURÉE OF RUTABAGAS AND POTATOES
(SERVES 6)

3 *small rutabagas (about 1½ pounds), washed, peeled, and cut in cubes*
2 *Idaho baking potatoes, washed, peeled, and cut in cubes*
Salt to taste
¼ *cup heavy or light cream*
3 *tablespoons butter*
2 *tablespoons chopped parsley*

Prepare the rutabagas and potatoes and cover each with cold water until you are ready to cook. Drain the rutabagas and place them in a large saucepan. Cover with fresh cold water, add a little salt, and bring to a boil. Cook until almost tender, or for about 30 minutes. Drain the potatoes and add them to the rutabagas. Continue cooking until both are tender. Drain thoroughly. Place the cream in an electric blender, add the vegetables, and blend until smooth. Reheat in a double boiler, add the butter, stir well, and serve at once—sprinkled lightly with chopped parsley. This goes well with Oven-Barbecued Spareribs (page 78).

WARM POTATO SALAD WITH COOKED SALAD DRESSING
(SERVES 6–8)

2 *pounds (about 6) medium-sized old potatoes*
Salt to taste
½ *teaspoon dill salt*
Pepper to taste

   2 *teaspoons finely chopped onion*
   1 *cup* Cooked Salad Dressing (*below*)
  ½ *cup heavy sweet cream*
   1 *teaspoon chopped parsley or, better still, finely cut dill*

Peel the potatoes, wash, and cover amply with cold water seasoned to taste with salt. Cook until tender through or for about
40 minutes. Drain well, and cut into bite-size pieces. While
still hot, sprinkle with the dill salt and pepper to taste. Add the
onion and Cooked Salad Dressing thinned with the heavy sweet
cream. Toss lightly with a fork and place in a salad bowl. Sprinkle with parsley or dill, and serve while still warm.

COOKED SALAD DRESSING
(1 CUP)

  2 *tablespoons all-purpose flour*
 ⅓ *teaspoon salt*
Scant ¼ *teaspoon pepper*
Scant ⅓ *teaspoon dry mustard*
  1 *tablespoon granulated sugar*
  2 *tablespoons butter*
  1 *whole egg, beaten to a froth*
 ⅓ *cup cider vinegar*
 ¼ *cup all-purpose cream*

Mix together the flour, salt, pepper, mustard, and sugar. Melt
the butter in the top part of a small enamel double boiler over
boiling water. Stir in the dry ingredients. Place the top part of
the double boiler over low heat and cook, stirring constantly
with a small wooden spoon, until well mixed and smooth. Remove from the heat, and stir in the beaten egg and vinegar.
Place back over boiling water and cook, stirring constantly, for

about 1 minute or until the dressing is thick and smooth. Remove from the heat entirely and stir in the cream. Refrigerate until ready to use.

POTATOES COLCANNON
(SERVES 4)

Preheat oven to 400°

    3 *medium-sized old potatoes (12 ounces when peeled)*
    2 *tablespoons butter*
    ¼ *cup hot light cream*
    1 *package (10-ounce) frozen leaf spinach*
    Salt and pepper to taste
    4 *hard-boiled eggs or 4 poached eggs*

Wash and peel the potatoes, cut into medium-size pieces, cover with cold water, and add ¼ teaspoon salt. Cook until they are tender through, or for about 25 minutes. Drain and mash the potatoes, add the butter and hot cream, and continue mashing until they are light and fluffy. Cook the spinach, following the directions on the package. Drain thoroughly, place in a sieve, and press with a spoon to eliminate as much juice as possible, then chop fine in a small wooden bowl. Add to the potatoes and mash until the potatoes and spinach are well mixed. Add salt and pepper to taste and pack the mixture into a well-buttered deep 3-cup mold. Place in the hot oven and allow to heat thoroughly, about 10 to 15 minutes, while you hard-boil or poach the eggs. Run a knife around the edge of the dish and turn out, like a mud pie, onto a hot serving dish. Garnish with sliced hard-boiled eggs and serve at once, or accompany this dish with poached eggs.

BRAISED CELERY
(SERVES 4)

Preheat oven to 400°

2 *bunches celery, pulled apart, washed, threads removed*
2 *slices bacon*
1 *small white onion, peeled and sliced*
1 *sprig parsley*
1 *pinch dried thyme*
1 *cup canned consommé, or substitute 1 teaspoon of Bovril broth*

Prepare the celery. Place the bacon in the bottom of a buttered rectangular oven-proof glass dish. Cover with sliced onion, and lay the celery on this bed. Tuck the parsley and thyme in one corner of the dish. Pour consommé or broth over all. Cover the dish with foil and bake for about ¾ hour. Serve hot.

MASHED PARSNIPS AND CARROTS
(SERVES 4)

6 *large fresh parsnips*
3 *or 4 large carrots*
½ *teaspoon salt*
1 *teaspoon sugar*
1 *quart water*
2 *tablespoons butter*

Wash and peel the parsnips, and split in two lengthwise. Split once more and cut out and discard the pithy cores. Slice crosswise. Wash and peel the carrots and slice crosswise. Combine the two vegetables in a pan, add salt, sugar, and the water. Bring to a boil and cook until tender, or for about 30 minutes, counting from the time they are actually boiling. Drain and mash together with a potato masher. Add butter and reheat the mixture over boiling water before serving.

NEW HAMPSHIRE STRING BEANS
(SERVES 4–6)

1 quart tender green string beans
1 tablespoon salt
1 tablespoon butter
⅛ teaspoon soda
1 teaspoon granulated sugar
1¼ teaspoons extra salt
Dash of pepper
1 cup boiling water or more
1 cup light cream

Wash the beans, break off both ends, and French them, using a gadget sold for the purpose. Place in a large enamel pan, cover with cold water, add 1 tablespoon salt, and allow to stand for 2 hours. Drain well. Put the butter in a saucepan and heat to a froth, but do not allow it to brown. Add the beans, soda, sugar, extra salt, and pepper. Cover with the boiling water, skim if necessary and cook gently until the beans are tender, or for about 30 to 45 minutes, or until almost all the juice has evaporated. Add the cream and allow to boil up once more. Serve immediately.

SUMMER SUCCOTASH
(SERVES 4)

1 *thick slice bacon cut in 1-inch pieces*
2 *cups shelled shell beans (rose-streaked ones)*
1 *small white onion, peeled and left whole*
3 *cups water (more if necessary)*
2 *cups fresh sweet corn (just cut off the cob)*
Salt to taste (about ½ teaspoon)
Dash of freshly ground black pepper
½ *cup heavy cream*

Place the bacon, beans, onion, and water in a 2-quart saucepan. Simmer until the beans are tender or for about 2 hours, adding more water if necessary. Add the corn and salt and pepper to taste. Bring to a boil, remove from the fire, and allow to stand covered for about 5 minutes. Add cream and serve.

BEETS WITH ORANGE SAUCE
(SERVES 4–6)

2 *pounds young tender beets*
⅓ *cup granulated sugar*
2 *tablespoons cornstarch*
Pinch of salt
1 *cup strained fresh orange juice*
2 *tablespoons butter*

Wash and cut off the leaves of the beets, leaving about 1 inch of the stems. Cook in boiling water until tender, or for about 40 minutes. Drain, drop in cold water for a moment, and pinch off the skins. Keep the beets warm while you make the orange sauce. Blend the sugar, cornstarch, and salt. Add the orange juice and butter. Cook in a double boiler until the sauce is rather thick. Pour over the beets and serve piping hot.

COTTAGER'S PROCERUS PIE
(SERVES 4)

Preheat oven to 350°

> ½ *pound fresh mushrooms*
> 1 *can (3-ounce) instant mashed potatoes*
> 1 ½ *cups boiling water*
> ⅔ *cup milk*
> 6 *tablespoons butter*
> 4 *strips bacon cut in 1-inch pieces*
> *Salt and freshly ground pepper to taste*

Wash and cut off the tough parts of the stems from the mushrooms. Slice fine. Follow directions on the can for making the mashed potatoes, using the water and milk, then beat in 2 tablespoons of the butter. Melt the rest of the butter in a frying pan, and when sizzling hot add the mushrooms and sauté them for about 5 minutes, stirring with a wooden spoon, but avoid allowing them to brown too much. Transfer to a 1-quart oven-proof baking dish. Without washing the frying pan, add the bacon and cook over moderate heat until lightly browned but not crisp. Cover the mushrooms with the bacon, sprinkle with pepper and cover with the mashed potatoes. Season to taste with salt. Bake in the preheated oven until lightly browned, or for about 20 minutes.

BAKED CORN
(SERVES 6–8)

Preheat oven to 375°

> 24 *large ears fresh-picked corn*
> 1½ *teaspoons salt*
> ¼ *teaspoon coarsely ground pepper*
> 1 *tablespoon granulated sugar*
> ½ *pound butter and more*

Butter copiously two 9½-inch oven-proof glass pie plates. Husk the corn. With a sharp knife score each row of kernels, slice off a thin layer, and then scrape well with the dull side of the knife to extract all the remaining milky pulp. You should have about 8 cups pulp. Season with the salt, pepper, and sugar. Cut the butter in thin slices and mix with the corn. Fill the pie plates and spread the corn out evenly, then bake for about 40 to 45 minutes, or until the sides and top are a crusty golden brown. Remove from the oven and serve.

ONIONS BAKED IN MILK
(SERVES 4)

Preheat oven to 450°

> 3 *cups very thinly sliced white onions (about 6–7 onions)*
> 1 *tablespoon flour*
> *Pepper to taste*
> 3 *tablespoons butter*
> 1 *cup whole milk*
> 1 *teaspoon salt*
> 1 *teaspoon chopped parsley*

Peel and slice the onions thin. Place in a deep oven-proof dish, sprinkle with flour, and stir with a fork to distribute the flour evenly. Sprinkle lightly with pepper. Dot with butter, and pour the milk over all. Bake in the preheated oven until the onions are soft and tender, or for about 45 minutes. Sprinkle with salt and parsley and serve at once.

DEVILED TOMATOES
(SERVES 4)

FOR THE SAUCE

> 1 *hard-boiled egg yolk rubbed through a sieve*
> 4 *tablespoons butter*
> 1 *scant tablespoon dry mustard*
> ¼ *teaspoon salt*
> 2 *teaspoons powdered sugar*
> 1 *big pinch cayenne*
> 1 *egg yolk*
> 2 *tablespoons cider vinegar*

First make the sauce. Hard-boil the egg and rub the yolk through a fine sieve. Melt the butter in the top part of a small double boiler over boiling water. Add the mustard, salt, sugar, and cayenne. Stir in the hard-boiled egg yolk, and when smooth add the raw egg yolk slightly beaten with the vinegar. Cook over boiling water until the sauce is slightly thickened, stirring constantly, for barely 1 minute. Remove from the lower part of the double boiler and set aside.

> 3 *large ripe tomatoes, cut in thick slices*
> ¼ *cup all-purpose flour (about)*
> *Salt and pepper to taste*

4 *tablespoons butter*
1 *tablespoon chopped parsley*

Wash the tomatoes, wipe dry and cut out a bit from the stem end of each. Cut crosswise in thick even slices. Season the flour with salt and pepper and place in a shaker. Spread the tomatoes out onto a sheet of waxed paper lightly floured with part of the seasoned flour. Sift the remainder of the flour over the tomatoes. Melt the butter in a large frying pan (preferably iron). Fry the tomatoes all at once, turning them over carefully with a spatula when browned on one side, or in about 5 minutes, and brown the other side.

Place on a large preheated platter and keep warm while you reheat the sauce for a second or two over boiling water. Spread over the tomatoes and sprinkle with the chopped parsley. Serve at once on hot plates. Crisp French or Portuguese or Italian bread goes well with these delicious tomatoes.

FRIED GREEN TOMATOES WITH MILK GRAVY
(SERVES 4–6)

Preheat oven to 350°

4 *large green tomatoes*
¼ *cup light-brown sugar*
½ *cup fine dry bread crumbs*
¾ *teaspoon salt*
Dash of freshly ground pepper
6 *tablespoons butter* (*about*)
2 *tablespoons flour*
1 *cup or more whole milk*

Wash the tomatoes and remove a small slice from both ends of each. Slice crosswise in pieces ½ inch thick. Mix together in a soup plate the sugar, crumbs, salt, and pepper. Press both sides of the slices into the crumb mixture. Heat a very large iron frying pan over low heat, add 2 tablespoons of the butter, and when sizzling hot add as many slices of the tomatoes as will fit comfortably. Have ready in the oven an oven-proof platter or pan. Cook the tomatoes gently for about 10 minutes, and turn them over with a pancake turner. Cook another 10 minutes on the second side and place in the oven while you repeat the process, until all the slices have been fried, adding more butter to the frying pan as required.

If a milk gravy is desired, sprinkle the flour over the residue in the frying pan, stir well with a wooden spoon, and gradually add the milk until the gravy is of the desired consistency. Serve the gravy separately in a gravy boat, and send the brown tomatoes to the table.

BAKED TOMATOES STUFFED WITH CORN PUDDING
(SERVES 6)
Preheat oven to 350°

      6 *large ripe tomatoes, well washed*
      9–10 *ears of fresh sweet corn, husked*
      1 *large egg, separated*
      1 *tablespoon butter, melted*
      1½ *teaspoons granulated sugar (about)*
      ¾ *teaspoon salt*
      1½ *tablespoons soft butter*
      Paprika

Cut the tops off the tomatoes and scoop out the pulp and seeds.

Reserve for another use. Turn the tomatoes upside down on a plate to drain while you are preparing the pudding. With a sharp knife slit down the center of each row of kernels, and with the dull edge of the knife push out the juice onto a plate. This should give you about 1½ cups pulp. Place this in a bowl. Stir in the unbeaten egg yolk and the melted butter, and season to taste with the sugar and salt. Beat the egg white until stiff and fold in. Butter a baking dish just large enough to hold the six tomatoes upright. Fill them with the pudding mixture. Dot with the soft butter and sprinkle copiously with paprika. Bake in the preheated oven for about 45 minutes or until the pudding is puffed and golden brown. Serve at once.

TRANSPARENT DRESSING FOR RAW TOMATOES
(SERVES 6–8)

½ *cup granulated sugar*
1 *teaspoon dry mustard*
1 *teaspoon salt*
½ *teaspoon celery seed, or more*
¾ *teaspoon paprika*
3 *tablespoons white wine vinegar or cider vinegar*
1 *teaspoon onion juice*
1 *cup vegetable oil*

Mix all together except the oil, then add it, a small amount at a time. Beat well. The dressing will become thick and shiny. Poured over sliced ripe tomatoes just before serving, it makes them shiny and pretty, and is delicious, I think.

STUFFED EGGPLANT
(SERVES 4)

Preheat oven to 375°

    1 medium-sized eggplant, pulp coarsely chopped
    1 package frozen mushrooms in butter sauce
    ⅓ pound (4 thin slices) Danish cooked ham
    2 small white onions, chopped fine
    7 tablespoons butter
    ¼ teaspoon salt (about)
    Dash of pepper
    ½ cup dry bread crumbs
    ¼ cup water
    Several strips of red pimiento

Cut the eggplant in two lengthwise and remove the stem end. With a sturdy teaspoon, scoop out the pulp to within ½ inch of the outer skin, and chop the pulp coarsely. Cook the mushrooms, following the directions on the package. When done, chop coarsely. Mince the ham in the electric blender while you count 4. Peel and chop the onions fine. Melt 4 tablespoons of the butter in a frying pan, add the onions, mushrooms, and eggplant and cook over moderate heat for about 10 minutes, stirring occasionally with a wooden spoon. Stir in the minced ham and season to taste with the salt and pepper. Fill the two eggplant shells with the mixture. Melt the remaining 3 tablespoons butter and stir in the bread crumbs. Spread evenly over the stuffing in the eggplant halves. Place them in a shallow baking dish and pour the water around them. Bake in the preheated oven for about 25 to 30 minutes or until the mixture is a golden brown on top. Garnish with several strips of pimiento and send to the table.

EGGPLANT FRITTERS
(SERVES 4)

1 small firm eggplant weighing about 1 pound
3¾ teaspoons salt
1 quart boiling water (about)
¼ cup all-purpose flour
1 teaspoon baking powder
1 egg, well beaten
1 tablespoon milk, about
½ pound pure lard or more
Confectioner's sugar

Wash, stem, and peel the eggplant. Slice thin, and put it to soak for 1 hour in cold water to cover in which you have dissolved 3 teaspoons of the salt. Drain well and place it in an enamel pan. Sprinkle with an additional ¾ teaspoon salt and cover with about 1 quart boiling water. Cook until the eggplant is soft, or for about 15 minutes. Drain again, pressing well with a spoon to extract the water, and mash with a potato masher until smooth. Sift together the flour and baking powder, and sift again into the mashed eggplant. Stir well and add the well-beaten egg and just sufficient milk to make a batter consistency.

Melt the lard over moderate heat until it registers about 360° to 370°, or deep-fat-frying temperature. Drop the mixture by tablespoonfuls into the fat and cook 3 or 4 fritters at a time, turning them over with a sieve spoon to brown both sides equally, or for about 1 minute in all. Drain on paper toweling and continue until all the batter has been used, making in all about 10 fritters. Place on a hot platter, sprinkle copiously with confectioner's sugar and serve at once.

CREAMED CUCUMBERS
(SERVES 4)
2 *large tender cucumbers*
3 *cups boiling water*
¾ *teaspoon salt*
3 *tablespoons flour*
3 *tablespoons butter*
1½ *cups hot whole milk*
Additional salt to taste
Dash of pepper

Wash the cucumbers, peel, and cut in two lengthwise. Remove any large seeds, and cut crosswise in 1-inch pieces. Cover with the boiling water, add the salt, and cook until tender, or for 10 to 15 minutes. Drain well.

Now make the cream sauce as follows: Melt butter and combine with flour in the top part of a double boiler, over low heat, stirring constantly for a minute or two with a wooden spoon. Gradually add the hot milk, stirring furiously to make a smooth sauce. Place over boiling water, cover, and continue cooking, about 10 to 15 minutes longer. Add the drained cucumbers, additional salt to taste, and a dash of pepper. When the cucumbers are well heated through, place in a hot serving dish and serve.

VERMONT BAKED BEANS
(SERVES 6)

3 *cups pea beans*
½ *pound salt pork*
¾ *cup maple syrup*
3 *tablespoons sugar*
2 *teaspoons dry mustard*
1 *teaspoon salt*
1 *cup or more boiling water*

Soak the well-washed pea beans overnight in cold water. In the morning drain them, cover with fresh water, and bring slowly to a simmer. Cook until the skins burst when you take some on a spoon and blow on them. Scald ½ pound salt pork, cut in 2 pieces, and score the rind in 2 cuts about ½ inch deep. Put 1 piece of pork in the bottom of a beanpot. Drain the beans and put them in the pot. Mix together the maple syrup, sugar, dry mustard, and salt. Moisten with a cup of boiling water. Bury the second piece of pork, leaving just the rind exposed, and pour the mixture over all. Pour enough boiling water over all just to cover the beans. Cover the pot and bake in a slow (300°) oven for 8 hours, adding more boiling water if necessary. Half an hour before the beans are done, remove the cover and let them brown.

SHELL BEANS
(SERVES 4)

2 *pounds shell beans*
6 *strips lean bacon cut in 1-inch pieces*
2 *tablespoons butter*

Boiling water as needed
2 tablespoons granulated sugar
½ teaspoon salt
1 tablespoon chopped parsley

Shell the beans, and wash in cold water. Render the pieces of bacon in a frying pan, cooking slowly, until almost but not quite crisp. Drain off the fat. Add the butter and the beans and cover with boiling water, about 3 cups. Add sugar and salt and simmer gently for about 2 hours, or until the beans are very tender, adding additional boiling water as needed to keep the beans constantly barely covered. When the beans are done, place in a hot vegetable dish, sprinkle with parsley, and serve.

FOUR-BEAN SALAD
(SERVES 8)

2 cups cooked string beans
2 cups cooked yellow wax beans
1 one-pound can well-drained kidney beans
2 cups cooked fresh lima beans
1 green pepper, seeds removed, sliced paper thin
1 peeled raw onion, sliced thin
1 tablespoon chopped fresh tarragon
Crisp, well washed Boston lettuce leaves, well drained

Make a salad dressing using:
½ cup granulated sugar
½ cup red-wine vinegar
½ cup olive or peanut oil
Scant teaspoon salt
½ teaspoon dry mustard

Pour the dressing over the combined beans, toss well, cover, and marinate several hours, stirring once or twice. When ready to serve, line a chilled salad bowl with lettuce leaves. Drain the beans and place on the bed of lettuce. Sprinkle with chopped fresh tarragon and serve.

COLE SLAW
(SERVES 6–8)

4 *cups finely shredded cabbage*
½ *cup diced peeled young cucumbers*
½ *cup diced hearts of celery (strings removed)*
¼ *cup chopped sweet green pepper*

Mix all above ingredients and chill well. Then blend with a dressing made of:

½ *cup mayonnaise*
2 *tablespoons cider vinegar*
2 *teaspoons prepared mustard*
Salt to taste

Toss lightly together. This will go nicely with grilled frankfurters on toasted buns, but with any number of other meats, too.

SIX

Puddings & Custards

SUSAN'S PLUM PUDDING
(SERVES 8–12)

4 ounces or about 5 cups fresh white bread, crusts removed, pulled apart

10 ounces or 2 cups light-brown sugar (well packed)

10 ounces or 2½ cups mashed and dried currants

10 ounces or 2¾ cups seeded raisins

10 ounces or 3½ cups beef suet, put through a grinder or chopped fine

10 ounces candied orange peel, lemon peel, and ginger, cut fine, in the proportion of about ¼ cup ginger, ¾ cup lemon peel, and ¾ cup orange peel, or 1¾ cups in all

3 tablespoons powdered cinnamon

1 teaspoon grated nutmeg

1½ teaspoons powdered cloves

1 teaspoon salt

½ pint brandy and more

1 scant cup molasses

1 *cup all-purpose flour*
2 *medium apples, peeled and chopped*
4 *eggs, beaten well*

Put everything together in a large bowl and let stand overnight. The next morning butter a 6-cup melon mold and two 4-cup molds. Pack the molds ⅔ full with the pudding mixture. Lay a small square of buttered and floured white cloth over each. Cover tightly, place the molds on a rack in a steamer, and surround with boiling water, so that the molds are more than half immersed. Cover the steamer and steam 6 hours, adding more boiling water as necessary. A roasting pan with its cover will do if you have no steamer.

When the puddings are done, remove the molds from the water and cool. When cold, remove from molds, and wrap the puddings in several thicknesses of cheesecloth. Tie securely with white string. Saturate with brandy, wrap again in heavy foil, and tie with string, until you are ready to steam them again before serving.

An hour or more before serving time place a pudding, still wrapped in cheesecloth, in a colander over boiling water in a suitable kettle. Cover tightly and steam for at least an hour. Turn out on a deep serving platter, remove the cheesecloth, place a sprig of holly on top of the pudding, pour warmed brandy over the pudding, light it, and send the pudding blazing to the table, accompanied by Hard Sauce (page 124) or Foamy Sauce.

FOAMY SAUCE
(About 2 cups; SERVES 6–8)
½ *cup butter at room temperature*
1 *cup confectioner's sugar*
1 *egg, well beaten*

2 *tablespoons brandy or sherry*
½ *cup heavy cream, whipped*

Cream the butter and gradually add the sugar. Beat the egg well and add to the butter and sugar. Place in the top part of a double boiler over boiling water and add the brandy or sherry. Beat constantly with a rotary beater until the mixture thickens and becomes hot and foamy, or for about 10 minutes. Remove from the heat and fold in the whipped cream. Place in a serving bowl and serve at once while still warm.

FANCY BREAD PUDDING
(SERVES 6)

Preheat oven to 375°

1 *teaspoon vanilla*
Pinch of salt
3 *additional tablespoons sugar for meringue topping*
¼ *teaspoon cream of tartar*
¾ *cup orange marmalade*
½ *cup blanched slivered almonds, lightly toasted*
4 *slices white bread, crusts removed*
3 *eggs, separated*
½ *cup granulated sugar*
1 *cup milk*
1 *cup light cream*
1 *cup heavy cream, slightly beaten*

Cut the bread in equal-sized squares, making 16 pieces. Put these in a saucepan. Beat the egg yolks until light, gradually adding the sugar. Stir in the milk and light cream, and flavor with ½ teaspoon of the vanilla. Pour over the bread and soak 10 minutes. Pour into a round 1½-quart oven-proof dish. Place the dish in a shallow pan and surround with hot water. Bake in the preheated oven until the pudding tests done in the center, or for about 50 to 55 minutes.

Beat the whites of eggs with a pinch of salt until stiff, add the 3 additional tablespoons sugar gradually, beating constantly. Flavor with the remaining ½ teaspoon vanilla. Add the cream of tartar and continue beating until very stiff.

Now spread the pudding with the marmalade, and sprinkle with the toasted almonds. Cover the entire surface with the meringue, spreading it evenly, then with the tip of a teaspoon make a pretty pattern. Place the pudding back in the hot oven and bake until the meringue is lightly browned, or for 8 to 10 minutes. Serve while still warm, accompanied by the slightly beaten heavy cream.

CHOCOLATE BREAD PUDDING
(SERVES 4)

Preheat oven to 325°

  2 *slices stale white bread, crusts removed*
  2 *cups milk*
  2 *ounces sweet chocolate*
  ½ *teaspoon powdered cinnamon*
  ¼ *cup granulated sugar*
  Pinch of salt
  1 *large egg*
  1 *teaspoon vanilla*
  1 *cup heavy cream* (*whipped until almost stiff*)

Butter a 1-quart baking dish. Crumble the bread into a mixing bowl. Heat the milk and chocolate together on very low heat, stirring constantly. When the chocolate has completely melted, remove from the heat and beat with a rotary beater, about 1 minute. Stir the cinnamon into the sugar, along with the salt. Add this to the hot chocolate and stir well. Beat the egg in a separate bowl and add it to the hot chocolate mixture, and stir in the vanilla. Pour the whole onto the bread crumbs, and when well mixed pour into the buttered baking dish. Place the dish in a shallow pan of hot water and place in the preheated oven to cook slowly for about 55 minutes. Remove from the hot water and cool. When the pudding is cold, refrigerate it until well chilled. Serve with whipped cream.

Note: The pudding may also be served hot as it comes out of the oven.

DELICATE INDIAN PUDDING
(SERVES 6)

Preheat oven to 350°

> 1 *quart milk*
> 4 *tablespoons white cornmeal*
> 3 *eggs*
> 4 *tablespoons sugar*
> 1 *scant teaspoon salt*
> ½ *teaspoon powdered ginger*
> 1 *tablespoon light molasses*
> 1 *tablespoon butter*
> 1 *cup cream*

Heat the milk in the top part of a double boiler over boiling water. Add the cornmeal gradually, stirring constantly. Cook about 12 minutes or until thickened, stirring occasionally. Beat together the eggs, sugar, salt, ginger, and molasses. Stir the butter into the milk and meal until it is melted, then pour gradually onto the egg mixture. Pour into a lightly buttered 1½-quart oven-proof dish, and bake slowly, about 50 to 60 minutes. Serve hot with cream.

SHIRLEY'S PRETTY SNOW PUDDING WITH CUSTARD SAUCE
(SERVES 6)

1 *envelope plain gelatin*
¼ *cup cold water*
1 *cup boiling water*
1 *cup granulated sugar*
¼ *cup strained lemon juice (2 lemons)*
3 *large egg whites*
2 *cups Soft Thick Custard Sauce (page 117)*
Ice cubes and white blossoms, for decoration

Soak the gelatin for 5 minutes in the cold water. Add the boiling water, sugar, and lemon juice. Stir until the sugar has dissolved. Cool and refrigerate until amost set, or for about 2 hours. Beat the egg whites until stiff, set aside, and with the same beater beat the gelatin mixture until white and frothy. Add the egg whites and continue beating over ice water until the pudding is snow white and almost stiff. Place in a 5-cup round mold, rinsed in cold water. Refrigerate.

When you are ready to serve, turn out onto a not-too-deep round serving dish, nestled into another dish. Surround the pudding dish with ice cubes among which you have planted white blossoms of one kind or another, rose of Sharon being an ideal choice. Send to the table accompanied by well-chilled Soft Thick Custard Sauce. A very pretty dessert.

SOFT THICK CUSTARD SAUCE
(About 2 cups; SERVES 6)
2 *cups milk*
3 *tablespoons granulated sugar*
Yolks of 3 *eggs*
1 *teaspoon cornstarch*
1 *teaspoon vanilla extract*

Heat the milk in the top part of an enamel double boiler over boiling water. Add the sugar and stir. Beat the egg yolks and cornstarch together in a small bowl. Add a little of the hot milk and stir well, then add gradually to the hot milk. Cook until well thickened, stirring constantly, or for about 5 minutes. Cool, add vanilla, and refrigerate until you are ready to serve.

RICE CUSTARD
(SERVES 6)
½ *cup long-grain rice, well washed*
2 *quarts boiling water*
1 *teaspoon salt*
3 *cups milk*
5 *tablespoons granulated sugar*
4 *egg yolks*
1 *teaspoon vanilla*
¼ *teaspoon lemon extract*
¾ *cup seedless raisins, soaked* 10 *minutes in* 1 *cup hot water*

Cook the rice in the boiling water with the salt added until just tender, or for about 18 minutes. Drain well. Heat the milk and sugar together in the top part of a double boiler over boiling water. Beat the yolks well, add a small quantity of the hot milk to the yolks and mix well, then add gradually to the hot milk, stirring constantly. Cook until the custard coats a silver spoon, or for about 5 minutes. Cool and flavor with the vanilla and lemon extract. In the meantime soak the raisins, drain, and dry on paper toweling. Add the raisins to the custard and stir in the well-drained rice. Serve warm or cold, as preferred.

CREAMY BAKED RICE PUDDING
(SERVES 6–8)

Preheat oven to 250°–275°

> ⅓ *cup long-grain uncooked rice*
> ¾ *cup granulated sugar*
> ½ *teaspoon salt*
> ½ *teaspoon grated lemon peel*
> 6 *cups whole milk*
> 1 *cup seedless black raisins*
> 1 *teaspoon vanilla*
> *Pitcher of light or heavy cream*

Wash the rice thoroughly in cold water, drain, and sprinkle over the bottom of a well-buttered 2-quart baking dish. Add the sugar, salt, and lemon peel, and pour the milk over all. Bake for an hour, stirring with a fork every 20 minutes. Continue baking another 2 hours, stirring occasionally. An hour before the pudding will be done, add the raisins. Stir well whenever a brown film forms on top. Before stirring for the last time, add the vanilla. Serve hot with cream.

IRISH-MOSS BLANCMANGE
(SERVES 6)
Large handful Irish moss (freshly gathered)
1 quart whole milk
⅓ cup sugar
Pinch of salt
¾ teaspoon lemon extract (about)
Pitcher of light or heavy cream

Wash the moss thoroughly in cold water, discarding all unattractive bits. This should give you 1 cup moss. Wash once more to be sure the moss is clean and free from sand. Place it in a saucepan and add the milk, sugar, and salt. Bring slowly to the boiling point, stirring constantly, but do not boil it. Remove from the heat and strain through a fine sieve. Discard the moss and partially cool the milk. Flavor to taste with the lemon extract, pour into 6 custard cups (¾-cup size), and refrigerate until well chilled and set. Serve with the cream.

Note: The sea moss may be gathered along parts of the New England shore or it may be purchased in certain drugstores.

GRAPENUT CUSTARD
(SERVES 6)
Preheat oven to 350°–375°
3 cups whole milk
⅔ cup granulated sugar
Pinch of salt
½ cup Grapenuts
3 whole eggs
1 teaspoon vanilla

Place the milk in the top part of an enamel double boiler over hot water. Stir in the sugar, salt, and Grapenuts. Heat to the scalding point, stirring occasionally. Remove from the heat and cool partially. When cooled, beat the eggs well and stir into the milk. Add vanilla and pour into six ¾-cup custard cups. Place the cups in a shallow pan of hot water and bake for about 40 to 45 minutes or until the custard is set through. Cool and serve lukewarm or refrigerate and serve cold.

MOLDED CORNSTARCH BLANCMANGE
(SERVES 4)

½ cup granulated sugar
5 tablespoons cornstarch
¼ teaspoon salt
1 quart whole milk
1½ teaspoons vanilla
½ teaspoon almond extract
2 boxes frozen raspberries, defrosted

Mix the sugar, cornstarch, and salt in the top part of an enamel double boiler. Gradually add the milk, stirring until smooth. Place over boiling water and cook, stirring constantly, until the mixture thickens. Cover and continue cooking for 10 minutes or longer, stirring occasionally. Remove from the heat and stir in the vanilla and almond extract. Rinse a 1-quart melon mold with cold water and fill with the blancmange mixture. When it is cold, cover, and refrigerate until well chilled, at which time run a knife around the edge and turn out into an oval dessert dish. Send to the table accompanied by a separate bowl of defrosted raspberries.

MISS FOLSOM'S LAND-OF-THE-SKY PUDDING
(SERVES 4)
1 *envelope plain gelatin*
¼ *cup cold water*
¾ *cup boiling water*
1-*pound jar cooked prunes, pitted and cut in half*
1 *cup heavy cream, whipped*

Soak the gelatin in the cold water for 15 minutes. Stir in the boiling water. Mix well and pour into a shallow rectangular dish about 3 inches by 6½ inches. Refrigerate several hours until well set. Put the prunes and their juice in a pretty serving dish and chill. When you are ready to serve, cut the gelatin in equal-sized squares, making 40 squares. With the aid of a small spatula, place the squares over the prunes, keeping them in as perfect squares as possible. Whip the cream and cover the whole with this white topping. Serve at once.

PORTUGUESE SWEET RICE
(SERVES 4)
2½ *cups whole milk*
¼ *teaspoon salt*
½ *cup Cream of Rice cereal*
⅜ *cup granulated sugar*
⅓ *cup finely ground blanched almonds*
¼ *teaspoon lemon extract*
¼ *teaspoon vanilla extract*
¼ *teaspoon orange-flower water*

2 *tablespoons cream* (*optional*)
1 *cup heavy cream or stewed fruit*

Scald the milk and salt in the top part of an enamel double boiler over boiling water. Gradually stir in the Cream of Rice cereal. Cook for a minute or two, stirring constantly, then cover and continue cooking 4 or 5 minutes longer, stirring once or twice. Stir in the sugar and the almond powder and, last of all, the three flavorings. Cook one minute longer. Remove from the heat and serve warm or cold with fruit or cream. If the pudding is to be served cold, cover the top with 2 tablespoons cream to prevent hardening and chill. Turn out into a dessert bowl, surround with any desired stewed fruit, and serve. A pitcher of cream may be substituted for the fruit.

STEWED FRESH PEACHES FOR THE PORTUGUESE SWEET RICE
(SERVES 4–6)
¾ *cup granulated sugar*
½ *cup water*
6 *large peaches*

First moisten the sugar with the water and bring to a boil. Skim carefully and cook five minutes. In the meantime dip the peaches one by one into boiling water for a second or two, then plunge into cold water. The skins may then be easily removed, leaving the peaches smooth and pretty. Slice the well-drained peaches into crescent-shaped pieces and add them to the hot syrup. Bring to a boil, remove from the heat, and cool. Then refrigerate until well chilled.

BLUEBERRY PUDDING WITH HOT BLUEBERRY
SAUCE AND HARD SAUCE
(SERVES 6–8)

Soft butter for buttering mold
1½ cups blueberries
2½ cups all-purpose flour
¼ cup soft butter
¾ cup granulated sugar
1 egg, well beaten
½ teaspoon vanilla extract
½ teaspoon lemon extract
½ teaspoon baking soda
1 cup buttermilk
Boiling water
Hot Blueberry Sauce (below)
Hard Sauce (below)

Butter a 1-quart mold copiously, including the inside of the lid. Pick over and wash the blueberries, and dry thoroughly on several thicknesses of paper toweling. Flour them lightly, using a tablespoon or more of the flour. Cream the butter with the sugar until light and fluffy. Beat the egg and stir into the butter and sugar. Add the flavoring. Add the soda to the buttermilk, stir well, and add it alternately with the remainder of the flour to the butter, egg, and sugar mixture, making a smooth dough. Fold in the floured blueberries.

Pack smoothly into the mold, cover securely with the lid, and place the mold, round side down, on a rack in a pot large enough to hold it comfortably. Pour around the mold sufficient boiling water to reach the level of the bottom of the lid. Cover the pot and steam for three hours, replacing the boiling water as needed. When the pudding is done, lift the mold carefully from the boiling water. Remove the lid from the mold, run a knife around the pudding, and turn out onto the center of a large, deep oval serving dish. Surround the pudding with the Hot Blueberry Sauce, and serve at once, accompanied by Hard Sauce in a separate sauceboat.

HOT BLUEBERRY SAUCE
(SERVES 6–8)
3 *cups blueberries, picked over and washed*
1½ *cups granulated sugar*
1 *teaspoon powdered cinnamon*

Place the berries, washed and drained, in a deep saucepan. Add the cinnamon to the sugar and stir into the berries. Place on a low flame and stir constantly until they form their own juice and are boiling in it. Continue cooking, watching carefully to prevent sticking, and in about 10 to 15 minutes they should be done. Serve hot with Blueberry Pudding.

HARD SAUCE
(SERVES 6–8)
½ *cup butter, at room temperature*
1¼ *cups superfine sugar*
Pinch of nutmeg
1 *teaspoon vanilla*
¼ *teaspoon lemon extract*

Cream the soft butter, gradually adding the sugar. When the mixture is light and fluffy, add the flavoring, stir well, and place in a serving dish. Cover, and chill until ready to serve.

RICE MOLD WITH MAPLE SUGAR
(SERVES 6)

Preheat oven to 450°

2 *teaspoons salt*
1 *cup rice, well washed*
3 *pints boiling water*
½ *cup whole milk*
¼ *cup heavy cream*
¼ *pound sweet butter*
½ *cup or more scraped or granulated maple sugar*
Extra heavy cream, if desired

Add the salt and the well-washed and drained rice slowly to the boiling water, so that the water never stops boiling. This takes about 3–4 minutes. Continue cooking until the grains of rice are tender through, or for about 18 minutes. Drain well. Place in an enamel saucepan and add the milk and heavy cream. Place on very low heat and cook, stirring frequently, until all the milk and cream have been absorbed, or for about 10 minutes. Watch carefully to avoid scorching.

Transfer the mixture to a well-buttered quart mold, pressing it well in. Cover and place the mold in the preheated oven for about 5 minutes. Run a knife around the edge and turn out carefully onto a hot serving dish. Serve hot, with plenty of sweet butter and scraped or granulated maple sugar. Heavy cream may also be served, if desired.

CHARLOTTE RUSSE
(SERVES 6)

12 *ladyfingers* (*3-ounce package*)
1 *envelope plain gelatin*

¼ *cup cold water*
3 *eggs, separated*
3 *tablespoons granulated sugar*
1½ *cups milk*
2 *teaspoons vanilla*
1½ *cups heavy cream*

Pull the ladyfingers apart, making 24 halves. Line the bottom and sides of a deep rectangular mold, 5 inches by 9¼ inches by 2¾ inches, with the halves. Soak the gelatin in the cold water for 5 minutes. Beat the egg yolks until very light, adding the sugar gradually. Bring the milk to the boiling point and pour it into the egg yolks and sugar. Place in the top part of an enamel double boiler over boiling water and cook, stirring constantly until thickened. Add the gelatin and stir until the gelatin has been entirely dissolved. Place the pan over cold water and cool, stirring occasionally. When the mixture is cool stir in the vanilla.

Place in the refrigerator and watch carefully. In about 30 minutes it should have partially set. Now beat the whites of eggs, and when stiff, fold them into the gelatin mixture. Beat the cream until stiff and fold it into the mixture. Pour into the ladyfinger-lined mold and chill until well set. Turn out on a cold serving dish and serve cut in thick slices.

TRILBY PUDDING
(SERVES 6–8)

½ *pound shelled English walnuts (2 cups) coarsely chopped*
½ *pound fresh marshmallows*
2 *tablespoons powdered sugar*
1 *cup heavy cream, lightly beaten*
2 *teaspoons juice from maraschino cherries*
12 *maraschino cherries left whole for garnish*

Chop the walnuts but not too fine. Cut each marshmallow into 4 pieces with scissors dipped in cold water, dropping the pieces onto a plate sprinkled with powdered sugar, and roll the pieces around to keep them from sticking together. Whip the cream, not too stiff, flavoring it with the juice from the maraschino cherries. Mix all together and put into a pretty dessert serving bowl. Chill until ready to serve, at which time garnish with the whole cherries.

BAKED APPLE TAPIOCA
(SERVES 4–6)

Preheat oven to 375°

¼ cup granulated sugar

1 cup firmly packed light-brown sugar

2 tablespoon butter and more

½ teaspoon powdered cinnamon

¾ teaspoon salt

⅓ cup minute tapioca

3 tablespoons strained lemon juice (1 lemon)

2½ cups water

3 large firm tart apples, peeled, cored, and sliced fine

Pitcher of cream

Butter a large (2-quart) baking dish. Place the granulated and light-brown sugars in a deep pan. Add the butter, cinnamon, salt, tapioca, lemon juice, and water. Stir and place over low heat until the mixture comes to a boil. Set aside while you prepare the apples. Place them in the buttered baking dish and pour the tapioca mixture over them. Cover and bake in the preheated oven for about 35 minutes, stirring once or twice. Serve warm with cream.

STERLING PUDDING
(SERVES 6)

½ *cup milk*
½ *cup molasses*
2 *tablespoons melted butter*
1½ *cups flour*
½ *teaspoon baking soda*
½ *teaspoon salt*
½ *teaspoon powdered cinnamon*
¼ *teaspoon powdered cloves*
¼ *teaspoon grated nutmeg*

Butter a 1-quart pudding mold, including the lid. Mix together the milk, molasses, and melted butter. Sift together the dry ingredients. Sift them again gradually into the liquid mixture, beat until smooth, and pour into the mold. Cover tightly, place on a trivet in a deep kettle and pour around it sufficient hot water to reach halfway up the mold. Cover the pan tightly, place on high heat until it comes to a boil, reduce heat a bit and continue steaming two hours in all, replacing the boiling water as it boils down with more boiling water. Remove the mold from the water and cool slightly before turning it out onto a serving platter. Run a knife around the mold to loosen the pudding if it doesn't slip out easily. Serve while hot with Hot Lemon-and-Vanilla Sauce or with Vinegar Sauce.

HOT LEMON-AND-VANILLA SAUCE
(SERVES 6–8)

1 *cup granulated sugar*
2 *tablespoons cornstarch*

2 *cups boiling water*
¼ *pound butter*
Strained juice and grated rind of 2 large lemons
1 *teaspoon vanilla*

Mix together in a saucepan the sugar and cornstarch. Add the boiling water gradually, stirring constantly with a wooden spoon. Bring to a boil over low heat and continue cooking for 5 minutes, stirring constantly. Remove from the fire. Add the butter and stir until melted. Add the juice and grated rind of the lemons, and the vanilla. Serve hot on Sterling Pudding, or on Steamed Carrot Pudding (below).

VINEGAR SAUCE
(SERVES 6)

2 *cups granulated sugar*
⅔ *cup water*
1 *tablespoon cider vinegar*
1 *teaspoon vanilla extract*
½ *teaspoon nutmeg*

In a saucepan moisten the sugar with the water and vinegar. Place on a low flame and let it come to a lively boil. Add the vanilla and nutmeg, and allow it to cool. Refrigerate until you are ready to serve it on Sterling Pudding. The sauce may also be served hot if preferred.

REINHARDT'S STEAMED CARROT PUDDING
(SERVES 6–8)

1½ *cups seedless raisins*
1 *cup currants*

1   *teaspoon each powdered ginger, cinnamon, cloves, and nutmeg*
1   *teaspoon baking powder*
Dash of salt
1½ *cups all-purpose flour, unsifted*
1   *cup light-brown sugar, well packed*
1   *scant cup finely chopped fresh suet*
1   *cup grated raw carrots (4 medium-size)*
1   *cup grated raw potato (1 large)*

Butter a 1½-quart melon mold, including the inner side of the lid. Cut up some fresh suet, discarding all the thin membrane encountered. Chop very very fine in a wooden bowl. Measure out a scant cup of it. Wash and peel the carrots and grate them on the next to finest side of the grater. Do the same with the potato. Wash the raisins and currants in hot water and dry thoroughly on paper toweling. Add the spices, baking powder, and salt to the flour and sift once. Return the mixture to the sifter. Place the suet in a bowl, and add the brown sugar, grated carrots and potatoes, raisins, and currants. Sift in the spiced flour and mix well.

Pack into the buttered mold, pressing it in smoothly with a spoon. Cover tightly. Place the mold on a rack in a deep pan large enough to hold it comfortably and surround with boiling water, to about 1 inch from the top of the mold. Cover the pan and steam for 3 to 4 hours, adding more boiling water as it boils down. Remove the mold from the water. Wipe dry, remove the cover, and turn out onto a hot oval serving platter. Serve at once, accompanied by Hot Lemon-and-Vanilla Sauce (see page 128), Hard Sauce (see page 124), or Foamy Sauce (see page 112).

NEW ENGLAND APRICOT PUDDING
(SERVES 4–6)

Preheat broiling unit

> ½ *pound sun-dried apricots*
> 2 *cups water*
> ½ *cup granulated sugar*
> 8 *slices white bread*
> 2 *tablespoons soft butter*
> ¼ *cup sugar*
> ½ *teaspoon cinnamon*
> 1 *cup light or heavy cream*

Wash the apricots and soak them overnight in the water. Bring them gently to a boil the next morning and cook until tender, or for about 15 minutes. Remove from the heat and add the sugar and cinnamon. Stir lightly. Set aside.

Remove the crusts from the bread and cut into 8 pieces the correct size to line the bottom and sides of a small bread pan, 7½ inches by 3½ inches by 2 inches. Toast the bread lightly on both sides, and butter one side lightly, sprinkle with cinnamon sugar, and place under the broiler for a minute or two. Then reline the bread pan, placing the plain side next to the metal. Fill the center with the apricots and their juice. Cover and cool gradually. When you are ready to serve, turn the pudding out onto a small platter, cut at the table, and top with liquid or whipped cream.

SEVEN

Fruit Desserts & Other Sweets

APPLE DOWDY
(SERVES 6)

Preheat oven to 300°–325°

                6 *firm tart juicy apples*
                1 *cup light-brown sugar*
                ¼ *teaspoon nutmeg*
                ¼ *teaspoon salt*
                ½ *teaspoon cinnamon*
                2 *tablespoons sweet butter*
                ½ *cup warm water*
                1 *cup all-purpose flour*
                ¼ *teaspoon salt*
                2 *teaspoons baking powder*
                2 *tablespoons butter*
                Scant ½ cup milk
                Confectioner's sugar
                Pitcher of heavy cream

Wash, peel, quarter, and core the apples. Place in a baking dish 2½ inches deep by 8 inches in diameter. Sprinkle the brown sugar over the apples, and dust the top with the nutmeg, salt, and cinnamon. Dot with the butter and pour over all the warm water.

Now mix a baking-powder-biscuit dough. Sift the flour, salt, and baking powder into a bowl. Work the butter into this with your fingertips or a pastry cutter. Moisten with the milk. With floured hands gather the dough into a ball, and roll out on a heavily floured board or pastry cloth, to a circle slightly larger than the dish. Contrive to pick this up and place it squarely on top of the apples, pressing it to the rim of the dish. Make a large S-shaped incision in the center of the pie, with 6 or 8 extra slits around the edge. This is to allow the steam to escape while the pie is cooking. Place in a slow oven and bake slowly for about 3 hours. Sprinkle with confectioner's sugar and serve hot with plenty of cream.

APPLE OATMEAL SQUARES
(SERVES 6–8)

Preheat oven to 350°–375°

> 1 *cup all-purpose flour*
> ½ *teaspoon salt*
> ½ *cup light-brown sugar*
> ½ *teaspoon baking soda*
> 1 *cup quick-cooking oats*
> ½ *cup* (1 *bar*) *butter and more*
> 2 *or* 3 *large juicy apples*
> ½ *cup granulated sugar*
> ½ *pint light or heavy cream*

Butter copiously a 7-by-11-inch baking dish. Sift together the flour, salt, light-brown sugar, and baking soda. Stir in the oats.

With a pastry blender cut in ½ cup butter until the mixture is crumbly. Spread half the mixture evenly over the bottom of a baking dish. Wash, peel, quarter, and core the apples and slice them fine. Spread over the crumb mixture. Sprinkle with granulated sugar and dot generously with more butter. Cover the apples with the remainder of the crumb mixture. Bake in the preheated oven until the apples are soft and the crumb mixture is lightly browned on top, or for about 1 hour. Cut in squares and serve hot, with light or heavy cream.

APPLE SLUMP
(SERVES 4)

Preheat oven to 425°

> 5 *small McIntosh apples*
> ¼ *cup granulated sugar plus 2 tablespoons*
> *Powdered cinnamon*
> 1 *cup all-purpose flour*
> 2 *teaspoons baking powder*
> 3 *tablespoons soft salted butter plus 1 tablespoon*
> ½ *cup milk*
> 1 *cup heavy cream slightly whipped or Hard Sauce*

Butter copiously a 1-quart round oven-proof glass baking dish. Wash, peel, quarter, and core the apples. Place them in the dish. Cover with ¼ cup granulated sugar and sprinkle with cinnamon. Into a separate bowl sift together the flour, baking powder, and the additional 2 tablespoons sugar. Work 3 tablespoons butter into this with your fingertips. Moisten with the milk, mixing it lightly with a large fork. Drop by tablespoonfuls on top of the apples. Place in the preheated oven and bake until the biscuits are brown and the apples are sizzling in their juice, or for about 25 minutes. Turn out upside down onto a hot serving dish. Dot the apples with an additional tablespoon butter and sprinkle with the 2 tablespoons sugar and a light shower of cinnamon. Serve piping hot, accompanied by Hard Sauce (page 124) or slightly whipped heavy cream.

BLUEBERRY TOAST DESSERT
(SERVES 6)

Preheat broiling unit

> 6 *half-inch-thick slices of white bread*
> 2 *cups blueberries, carefully picked over*
> 1 *teaspoon lemon juice*
> ½ *cup granulated sugar*
> 1 *egg*
> Scant ¾ *cup milk*
> Pinch *of salt*
> ¾ *tablespoon butter*
> 2 *tablespoons confectioner's sugar*
> ½ *teaspoon powdered cinnamon*
> 1 *cup heavy cream*

Trim away the crusts from the bread, leaving about 2¾-inch squares. Wash the berries, place in a saucepan, add lemon juice and granulated sugar. Stir with a fork over a low flame until the sugar dissolves and the berries come to a boil. Cook 10 minutes, stirring occasionally. Pour into a rectangular oven-proof glass dish, 10 inches by 6 inches by 2 inches. Beat the egg, milk, and salt together. Heat the butter in a large 10½-inch frying pan. Dip the bread, both sides, into the egg mixture, one piece at a time, place in the sizzling butter and fry the bread until a golden brown on both sides, turning it over just once. Transfer with a pancake turner to the dish containing the blueberries, covering the berries neatly. Mix confectioner's sugar and cinnamon together and sprinkle evenly over the toast. Place under the broiler for a minute or two until the toast is lightly browned. Serve at once while hot, accompanied by a pitcher of heavy cream.

BLUEBERRY CRISP
(SERVES 6)

Preheat oven to 400°

> 2½ *cups large ripe blueberries*
> 1 *tablespoon lemon juice*
> ¾ *cup light-brown sugar (well packed)*
> ½ *cup unsifted all-purpose flour*
> ¼ *teaspoon salt*
> ¼ *teaspoon freshly grated nutmeg*
> *Generous ¼ cup butter at room temperature*
> ½ *pint heavy cream or vanilla ice cream*

Butter the sides and bottom of a 2-quart round baking dish. Pick over and wash the blueberries. Drain well. Place in the dish, spreading them evenly, and sprinkle with the lemon juice. Mix the brown sugar, flour, salt, and nutmeg; cut in the soft butter until the mixture is crumbly, using a pastry blender. Sprinkle evenly over the berries. Bake about 15 to 20 minutes or until bubbling. Cool slightly and serve warm with heavy cream or vanilla ice cream.

BLUEBERRY SLUMP
(SERVES 4–6)

Preheat oven to 350°

> 1 *quart blueberries*
> 1 *cup granulated sugar*

½ *teaspoon cinnamon*
Pinch of nutmeg
¼ *cup water*
1 *tablespoon fresh lemon juice*

Pick over and wash the berries. Place in a 2-quart round baking dish. Sprinkle with the sugar mixed with cinnamon and nutmeg. Moisten with the water and lemon juice. Stir lightly with a fork. Place in the preheated oven and bake 20 minutes, stir again, and cook about 10 minutes longer. Increase the heat of the oven to 425°–450° and remove the baking dish while you mix the biscuit dough.

FOR THE BISCUIT DOUGH

2 *cups all-purpose flour*
4 *teaspoons baking powder*
¼ *teaspoon salt*
2 *tablespoons granulated sugar*
4 *tablespoons butter*
4 *tablespoons pure lard*
About ¾ *cup milk*

Confectioner's sugar
1½ *cups light or heavy cream*

Sift the flour, baking powder, salt, and sugar into a bowl. Work the butter and lard into this with your fingertips or a pastry blender. Moisten to a soft dough consistency, using ¾ cup milk or slightly more. Drop by tablespoonfuls onto the hot blueberries. Return to the oven and bake until the biscuits have risen well and are a golden brown, or for about 30 to 35 minutes. Sprinkle with confectioner's sugar and serve while hot, accompanied by plenty of cream.

BLUEBERRY BUCKLE
(SERVES 8)

Preheat oven to 375°–400°

FOR THE CAKE

> ¼ *cup soft butter*
> ¾ *cup granulated sugar*
> 1 *egg, unbeaten*
> ½ *cup milk*
> 2 *cups sifted all-purpose flour*
> 2 *teaspoons baking powder*
> ½ *teaspoon salt*
> 2 *cups fresh or frozen unsweetened blueberries, defrosted*
> 2 *cups all-purpose cream or Custard Sauce (see page 141)*

Butter the sides and bottom of an 8-inch-square cake tin 2 inches deep. Cream the butter with the sugar, add the egg, and beat well. Add the milk alternately with the dry ingredients sifted together. Add the berries, mix them in carefully, and spread the mixture evenly in the pan. Top with the following topping mixture.

FOR THE TOPPING

> ¼ *cup soft butter*
> ½ *cup granulated sugar*
> ⅓ *cup sifted flour*
> ½ *teaspoon powdered cinnamon*

Blend the 4 ingredients together with a fork and distribute evenly over the cake dough. Place in the preheated oven and bake until the cake tests done in the center, or for about 35 to 40 minutes. Serve warm with Custard Sauce or cream.

BLUEBERRY ICE
(SERVES 4–6)

1 *pint blueberries, picked over and well washed*
1 *cup granulated sugar*
½ *tablespoon gelatin, dissolved in 2 tablespoons cold water*
1 *cup boiling water*
½ *cup fresh lemon juice*
1 *egg white*
½ *cup cold water (about), plus 2 tablespoons*

Put the berries in a bowl, sprinkle with ¼ cup granulated sugar, and crush well with a wire potato masher. Rub through a fine sieve with a wooden spoon. Discard what won't go through. Measure the resulting juice and add sufficient cold water to make 1½ cups. Soak the gelatin in 2 tablespoons cold water for 5 minutes. Bring 1 cup of water to a boil, and stir in the remaining ¾ cup sugar. Add the gelatin, blueberry pulp, and lemon juice, and stir well. When the mixture is cool, beat the egg white until stiff and stir it into the mixture until the whites disappear.

Place in a quart freezing tray and in the freezing compartment of the refrigerator. When the mixture is partially frozen, stir well, and when almost frozen stiff, scrape into a large bowl and beat until it turns light pink. Return to the freezing tray and continue freezing until you are ready to serve.

TO FREEZE BLUEBERRIES FOR FUTURE USE

Pick over, wash carefully in cold water, and place in plastic containers. Store in the freezing compartment of the refrigerator or in a deep freeze.

To freeze blueberries for fruit cup, etc., add a medium syrup to cover, and place in plastic containers in the freezing compartment of the refrigerator or in a deep freeze.

To make a medium syrup: Moisten 3 cups granulated sugar with 1 quart cold water. Bring to a boil, skim, and cook for a minute or two.

EUGENIE SHAW'S CRANBERRY TROLL CREAM VIA SHIRLEY CROSS
(SERVES 2)

This recipe is of Norwegian origin, but as cranberries are very New England, I'm including it.

> 1 *cup ripe perfect cranberries*
> 1 *tablespoon unbeaten egg white*
> ¼ *cup granulated sugar*
> 4 *ladyfingers*

Wash the cranberries, pick them over very carefully, and cut each in four if they are very tough-skinned. Place in the small bowl of an electric mixer. Add the egg white and sugar, and run at low speed for ¾ hour, scraping the sides of the bowl with a rubber spatula frequently. At first, nothing seems to happen, but gradually a delectable pink creamlike concoction takes form. The cranberries do not completely disappear, so, right or wrong, I rub the resultant pretty pink cream through a sieve, discarding the bits of cranberries still visible. Chill until you are ready to serve. Serve with ladyfingers.

CRANBERRY WHIP WITH CUSTARD SAUCE
(SERVES 6)

FOR THE WHIP

1½ cups ripe fresh cranberries
¾ cup water
1 envelope unflavored gelatin
¼ cup cold water
¾ cup granulated sugar
1½ teaspoons strained lemon juice
3 egg whites

Pick over the cranberries, wash, place in a pan, and cover with ¾ cup water. Bring to a boil and simmer, stirring occasionally, until the berries pop (about 8 minutes). Remove the pan from the stove and rub the berries through a fine sieve with a wooden spoon. Soften the gelatin with ¼ cup cold water, and add it to the hot cranberry mixture, stir in the granulated sugar, and stir until the gelatin and sugar are dissolved. Chill. Combine the lemon juice and whites of eggs in a large bowl and beat with a rotary beater until they are stiff but not dry. Add the cooled cranberry mixture, and beat with a rotary beater until light and fluffy. Rinse six ¾-cup custard dishes with cold water and fill to the brim with the whip. Chill. When you are ready to serve, run a knife around the edge of each and turn out into individual dessert dishes. Serve with custard sauce.

FOR THE SAUCE

3 egg yolks
3 tablespoons granulated sugar
½ teaspoon cornstarch
2 cups whole milk

>*½ teaspoon lemon extract*
>
>*Pinch of salt*

Beat the egg yolks and gradually add the sugar mixed with the cornstarch. Scald the milk in the top part of an enamel double boiler over hot water, and gradually stir in the egg mixture. Continue cooking until it coats a silver spoon, stirring constantly, about 5 to 6 minutes. Cool, and flavor with lemon extract and a pinch of salt.

COMPOTE OF RHUBARB, STRAWBERRIES, AND DRIED FIGS
(SERVES 6–8)

Preheat oven to 375°

>*1 pound (about 4 large stalks) tender pink rhubarb*
>
>*1 pint ripe strawberries (hulled and mashed)*
>
>*½ pound sun-dried figs*
>
>*1¼ cups granulated sugar*
>
>*1 cup water*
>
>*½ pint sour cream*

Wash the rhubarb, discarding the leaves and tip ends of stalks. Cut in 2-inch pieces. Wash and stem the strawberries, discarding any imperfect ones. Cut the dried figs in four with scissors, discarding stems. Place the rhubarb in a large (2-quart) deep, round oven-proof dish. Add the figs. Sprinkle with ¾ cup of the sugar and ½ cup of the water. Bake slowly for about 1 hour, basting every 15 minutes. In the meantime, in a saucepan, moisten the remaining ½ cup sugar with the remaining ½ cup water, bring to a lively boil, add the strawberries, and bring to a second boil. Skim carefully and continue cooking about 5 minutes longer. When the rhubarb and figs are cooked, pour the strawberries over them, cool and chill. Serve with sour cream.

FROZEN-FRUIT COMPOTE
(SERVES 6–8)

This recipe can be a substitute for the previous recipe when the fresh fruit is not available.

   1 package (1-pound) frozen rhubarb in sugar syrup
   1 package (1-pound) frozen strawberry halves in sugar
   1 jar (1-pound-1-ounce) whole figs in extra-heavy syrup
   1 jar (½-pint) sour cream
   ½ cup water

Defrost the strawberries. Bring the rhubarb to a full boil in a saucepan containing ½ cup water, over high heat. Separate the rhubarb with a fork to hasten thawing. Reduce the heat and boil gently until the rhubarb is tender, or for about 3 minutes. Add the contents of the package of frozen strawberries, but do not cook. Last of all, add the contents of the jar of figs and their juice. Cool and chill thoroughly before serving with sour cream.

A PARTY DESSERT
(SERVES 8)

   1 pound good marshmallows
   1 pint light cream
   ½ pound chopped walnut meats
   1 cup maraschino cherries, well drained and cut in four
   ½ cup canned pineapple, cut small
   1 teaspoon vanilla
   1 tablespoon sweet sherry

   1 pint heavy cream
   1 dozen almond macaroons

Place the marshmallows in the top part of a large enamel double boiler over boiling water and cover with the light cream. Stir over moderate heat for about 5 minutes, or until the marshmallows have melted. Remove from the fire and stir in the walnuts, cut cherries, and pineapple, and allow to cool. Add the vanilla and sherry. Beat the heavy cream until just barely stiff, then fold it into the rest. Place in a large mold which has been rinsed in cold water, cover, and refrigerate until set. When you are ready to serve, run a knife around the edge and turn out onto a chilled dessert dish. Serve on chilled plates and accompany with almond macaroons.

ALICE DOLBY'S STEWED PEARS
(SERVES 4)

Preheat oven to 400°

   8 small green pears, cut in two
   Strained juice of 1 lemon
   ½ cup granulated sugar
   ½ cup water
   Heavy cream

Wash the pears and cut in two lengthwise. Scoop out the cores and seeds, using a potato-ball cutter. Place side by side, cut side up, in a baking dish that will hold them comfortably. Sprinkle the pears with the lemon juice and sugar, distributing it equally. Pour the water around the pears. Cover the dish with foil, place in the preheated oven, and bake for about 1 hour, basting once or twice. Remove the cover and allow the pears to cook about

10 minutes longer, or until the pears and the juice begin to brown slightly. Serve hot or cold with heavy cream.

HOMEMADE CONCORD GRAPE GELATIN
(SERVES 3–4)

1 *quart homemade Concord grape juice (uncooked variety) (see p. 229)*
1 *envelope plain gelatin*

Open a quart jar of homemade Concord grape juice and strain, discarding the grapes. Soak the gelatin in ½ cup of the juice for 5 minutes. Heat 1½ cups of the remaining juice to the boiling point, skim, and stir in the soaked gelatin until dissolved. Pour into 3 or 4 custard cups (according to size), cool, and refrigerate until set.

GREENWICH, CONNECTICUT, WATERMELON
(SERVES 12)

1 *large watermelon*
2 *cups sugar*
1 *cup water*
1 *quart orange water ice*
1 *quart fine strawberries*
1 *pint raspberries*
1 *pint blackberries*
6 *apricots*
6 *ripe red plums*
4 *ripe peaches*
Confectioner's sugar
3 *dozen blanched almonds*

1 split of champagne, mixed with 2 tablespoons Curaçao (optional)

Cut a large watermelon in half lengthwise. With a large potato scooper, cut from the center of half of the watermelon 2 or 3 cupfuls of watermelon balls. Put them immediately in the refrigerator, and then with a big spoon remove the rest of the pulp from the same half, leaving a shell about 1¼ inches thick. Place the shell in the refrigerator or surround it with ice while you prepare the rest of the ingredients. First make a pitcher of syrup by boiling the sugar with the water for 5 minutes. Cool. When cold, pour a little over the watermelon balls. Wash and stem the strawberries, raspberries, and blackberries. Dry them on a cloth and place them in a bowl. Pour a little of the syrup over them and place in the refrigerator. Wash and quarter the apricots and plums, remove pits, and add a little syrup.

When ready to serve the watermelon, remove it from the refrigerator and empty the water ice into the center, squashing it to make an even bed over the bottom. On this bed arrange the different prepared fruits in stripes, alternating a light-colored fruit with a dark-colored one. The middle section is reserved for sliced peaches, which must be peeled, sliced, and sweetened at the last moment. The edge of the watermelon is sprinkled copiously with confectioner's sugar to make it look frosted. Sprinkle the top with blanched almonds. The well-chilled champagne-with-Curaçao may be poured on just before serving.

Because of the nature of this dish, it must be placed on the table and served from there, as it is too heavy to pass. This is a perfect dish for a hot summer day or night party in the garden.

EIGHT

Cakes & Tea Breads

RAISIN GINGERBREAD
(SERVES 6)

Preheat oven to 350°

⅔ *cup sugar*

⅔ *cup molasses*

⅔ *cup boiling water*

2 *tablespoons butter*

1 *teaspoon soda*

½ *cup raisins, washed and dried*

½ *cup chopped walnuts or pecans*

1 *egg, well beaten*

1½ *cups sifted flour*

1 *teaspoon cinnamon*

1 *teaspoon ginger*

¼ *teaspoon cloves*

1 *cup heavy cream, lightly beaten*

Mix together the sugar, molasses, and boiling water. While the mixture is still hot, stir in the butter and the soda. Cool. Add the raisins, nuts, and beaten egg. Sift together the flour and spices, and stir into the molasses mixture. Pour the batter into a well-buttered 9-inch-square cake pan and bake in the preheated oven for 35 to 40 minutes, or until it tests done in the center. Serve hot or cold with cream.

GRANDMOTHER'S CARAWAY-SEED POUND CAKE
(SERVES 6–8)

Preheat oven to 300°

> 1 *cup (2 bars) salted butter at room temperature*
> 1⅔ *cups granulated sugar*
> 5 *large eggs*
> 1 *teaspoon vanilla*
> *Grated rind of 1 lemon*
> 1 *tablespoon caraway seeds*
> 2 *cups sifted all-purpose flour*

Butter and flour a large bread pan. Place the soft butter in the bowl of an electric beater. Beat until light and creamy, then gradually beat in the sugar. When the mixture is light and fluffy, add the eggs, beating them in one at a time. Flavor with vanilla and lemon rind. Add the caraway seeds to the flour and fold it gradually into the batter. Place in a prepared large bread pan, and bake in a slow oven about 1½ to 1¾ hours, or until the cake tests done in the center. Turn out onto a cake rack to cool.

BLUEBERRY CAKE
(SERVES 6–8)

Preheat oven to 350°

    2 cans (15-ounce) wild blueberries in heavy syrup
    2½ cups all-purpose flour
    ½ teaspoon salt
    2½ teaspoons baking powder
    ½ cup butter
    1 cup granulated sugar plus ¼ cup
    1 egg
    ½ cup milk
    1 small piece cinnamon bark
    1 cup or more heavy cream

Butter a square 8-by-8-by-2-inch cake pan. Open the blueberries and strain, saving the juice. Sift together the flour, salt, and baking powder. Cream the butter and 1 cup of the sugar until light and fluffy. Beat the egg well, and beat it into the butter and sugar. Add the flour and milk alternately, making a smooth batter. Fold in the strained blueberries. Place in the cake pan, and bake in the preheated oven until the cake tests done, or for about 45 minutes.

In the meantime add the cinnamon and the extra ¼ cup sugar to the blueberry juice and boil down for about 15 minutes. Turn the cake out onto a large serving plate, and pour the reduced juice over all. Serve at once, cut in squares, with plenty of heavy cream.

KAY DRORBAUGH'S MOTHER'S FRUITCAKE
(4 SMALL LOAVES)

Preheat oven to 350°–375°

½ cup butter, and more
1 cup light-brown sugar
½ cup dark molasses
3 eggs, well beaten
1 cup brandy
1½ cups flour
½ teaspoon soda
1 teaspoon nutmeg
1 teaspoon allspice
1 teaspoon cinnamon
1 cup dates, pitted and cut small
1 cup figs, cut small
1 cup seedless raisins
1 cup currants
4 jars (4-ounce) Glacé Fruit Mix
1 cup almonds, blanched and sliced
1 cup walnut meats, chopped
Additional brandy

Butter four 7½-inch bread tins and line them neatly with heavy waxed paper. Cream the butter well, and add the sugar gradually. Stir in the molasses, beaten eggs, and brandy. Mix thoroughly. Sift together the dry ingredients and add with the nuts and fruits. When well combined, place in tins, and bake until firm to the touch, or for about 1½ hours. Cool, and wrap in cheesecloth saturated with brandy. Wrap in foil and refrigerate until ready to use, or store in a cool spot.

MAPLE-FROSTED LAYER CAKE
(SERVES 6–8)
Preheat oven to 375°

> 2 cups sifted cake flour
> 2½ teaspoons baking powder
> ½ cup salt butter
> 1¼ cups superfine sugar
> 1 teaspoon vanilla
> Pinch of salt
> 5 egg whites
> ½ cup milk

Butter and flour two 9-inch, round, straight-edged layer-cake tins. Sift together the flour and baking powder. Cream the butter and sugar until light and fluffy. Add the vanilla. Add the salt to the egg whites and beat until stiff but not dry. Add the sifted flour to the sugar and butter alternately with the milk. Lastly, fold in the whites. Put into the two cake tins and bake about 25 minutes, or until an inserted cake tester comes out clean. Turn out immediately onto cake racks to cool before putting together with Maple-Sugar Frosting, and covering sides and top smoothly.

MAPLE-SUGAR FROSTING
> 1 pound (2 cups) maple sugar
> 1 cup boiling water
> ¼ teaspoon cream of tartar
> 2 egg whites

Moisten the sugar with the boiling water and stir in the cream of tartar. Boil the syrup until it spins a thread from a spoon. Beat the egg whites stiff and pour the syrup slowly into the egg whites and continue beating until the frosting is thick enough to spread without running.

MAPLE UPSIDE-DOWN CAKE
(SERVES 4–6)

Preheat oven to 350°–400°

1 *cup pure maple syrup*
2 *tablespoons butter*
3 *tablespoons granulated sugar*
1 *large egg, well beaten*
1 *cup sifted flour*
2 *teaspoons baking powder*
¼ *teaspoon salt*
½ *cup milk*
12 *pecan halves*
½ *pint heavy cream*

Heat the syrup to the boiling point and pour into a rectangular oven-proof glass dish 10 inches by 6 inches by 2 inches. Cream the butter and sugar together, and stir in the well-beaten egg. Sift together the flour, baking powder, and salt, then sift again into the butter-sugar-egg mixture, adding the flour alternately with the milk to make a smooth batter. Pour onto the hot syrup, spreading it evenly.

Bake in the preheated oven until the cake is brown on top, and until it tests done in the center, or for about 25 to 30 minutes. Allow the cake to cool 10 minutes before turning it out bottom side up onto a hot platter, running a knife around the edge first to help loosen the cake. Dot with the pecan halves, cut into 6 equal portions, and serve while still warm, accompanied by heavy cream, slightly whipped or plain.

MAPLE TEA CAKES
(MAKES 12)
Preheat oven to 350°–375°

    1 cup granulated maple sugar
    ¼ cup granulated sugar
    ⅓ cup soft butter
    1 egg
    2 cups sifted cake flour
    ¼ teaspoon salt
    3 teaspoons baking powder
    ½ cup milk

Cream the sugars and butter together until light and smooth. Add the well-beaten egg. Sift the dry ingredients together and add alternately with the milk to the sugars and butter. Bake in well-buttered muffin tins until they test done, or for about 20 to 25 minutes. Turn out immediately onto a cake rack to cool.

BISHOP'S BREAD
(SERVES 6–8)
Preheat oven to 350°

    2 large eggs
    ½ cup granulated sugar
    1 teaspoon baking powder
    ¼ teaspoon salt
    ½ cup blanched, finely slivered almonds
    ¾ cup white raisins

½ *teaspoon vanilla*
Confectioner's sugar

Butter copiously a rectangular cake tin 11 inches by 7½ inches by 1½ inches. Separate the whites from the yolks of the eggs. Beat the yolks until light. Add the sugar gradually and continue beating until the mixture is very light and lemon-colored. Sift together the flour, baking powder, and salt. Stir into the egg mixture. Add nuts, raisins, and vanilla. Beat the egg whites until stiff and fold in. Spread evenly in the buttered pan. Bake until the cake tests done or for about 20 minutes. While still hot sprinkle copiously with confectioner's sugar. When cool cut into squares and serve.

SIMNEL CAKE
(SERVES 8)
For the fourth Sunday in Lent or "Mothering Sunday"
Preheat oven to 300°

FOR CAKE MIXTURE

1 *teaspoon grated lemon rind*
1 *teaspoon grated orange rind*
3 *pieces candied ginger, cut fine*
1 *teaspoon almond extract*
2 *tablespoons brandy*
¼ *teaspoon allspice*
1¾ *cups currants*
1½ *cups white seedless raisins*
4 *tablespoons (½ stick) butter*
¼ *cup granulated sugar*
4 *eggs, well beaten*

1 *cup ground blanched almonds*
½ *cup flour*
FOR ALMOND-PASTE FILLING
1 *8-ounce can almond paste*
1 *egg, well beaten*
1 *cup light-brown sugar*
2 *tablespoons brandy*
1 *teaspoon almond extract*
Confectioner's sugar

First, butter copiously a 9-inch round layer-cake tin (preferably one with a removable bottom), line the bottom with white paper, and butter the paper. Set aside while you make the cake mixture.

To make the cake mixture, cream the butter with the sugar and add the well-beaten eggs. Stir or beat until smooth. Add the ground almonds, flour, grated rinds, ginger, almond extract, brandy, allspice, and, last but not least, the currants and raisins. Set aside while you mix the Almond-Paste Filling.

Cut the almond paste into fine slices; then, using a small part of it, shape 12 small (½-inch) balls and set aside. To the remainder of the paste add the well-beaten egg and stir or beat until smooth. I accomplish this with the aid of my electric mixer. Add the brown sugar, brandy, and almond extract, and continue beating until very smooth and free from lumps.

Spread half of the cake mixture in the paper-lined cake pan, and cover with half of the Almond-Paste Filling. Then spread over the filling the remainder of the cake mixture. Place in the preheated oven and bake for about 1 hour and 15 minutes or until the cake is lightly browned on top and firm to the touch. Remove from the oven and cool slightly, then spread with the remainder of the Almond-Paste Filling. Reduce the heat of the oven to 200°. Place the reserved almond-paste balls evenly around the edge of the cake, 1 inch in from the rim, sprinkle the entire top lightly with powdered sugar, and bake until the top is lightly browned and the paste is set, or for about 10 to 15 minutes. Cool before serving and cut in thin, pie-shaped pieces.

LOUISE'S PARTY CHIFFON CAKE
(SERVES 6–8)

Preheat oven to 325°

> 7 *medium-size eggs*
> 2 *cups sifted all-purpose flour*
> 1½ *cups granulated sugar*
> 3 *teaspoons baking powder*
> 1 *teaspoon salt*
> ½ *cup vegetable oil*
> ¾ *cup cold water*
> 1 *teaspoon vanilla*
> ½ *teaspoon cream of tartar*
> ½ *cup confectioner's sugar*

Separate the yolks from the whites of the eggs. Sift the next 4 ingredients together into a large mixing bowl. Make a well in the center and add the vegetable oil, egg yolks, water, and vanilla. Beat until smooth for one minute with an electric beater. Add the cream of tartar to the egg whites and beat with another beater until they are very stiff and form peaks. *Do not underbeat.* Pour the first mixture into the egg whites and gently fold until well blended. *Do not stir.* Pour immediately into a large unbuttered tube pan. Bake 55 minutes at 325°, then increase heat to 350° and bake 10 to 15 minutes longer or until the cake springs back to the touch. Turn the pan upside down on a cake rack to cool. Run a spatula around the edge and center to loosen the cake and turn out onto the cake rack. Sprinkle copiously with confectioner's sugar before serving.

MASHED-POTATO CHOCOLATE CAKE
(SERVES 6–8)
Preheat oven to 375°

1 *cup hot mashed potatoes (made of 2 medium-sized potatoes, ¼ cup hot milk, and 1 tablespoon butter)*
¼ *pound (1 bar) butter at room temperature*
2 *cups granulated sugar*
3 *squares unsweetened chocolate, melted over hot, not boiling water*
1½ *teaspoons baking soda dissolved in ¼ cup water*
4 *large eggs, separated*
2 *cups cake flour*
2 *teaspoons baking powder*
½ *teaspoon salt*
½ *cup cold milk*
1 *teaspoon vanilla*

First make the mashed potatoes and keep hot over hot water. Butter well and flour two 9-inch round layer-cake tins. Cream the butter and sugar together until light. Add the hot mashed potatoes and the melted chocolate, and mix well. Add the dissolved baking soda, stir well, and add the egg yolks, beaten until very light. Sift together the flour, baking powder, and salt, and then sift the mixture again into the batter, adding it alternately with the cold milk, beating well with a spoon. Beat the egg whites until stiff. Stir in the vanilla and, last of all, fold the egg whites in carefully. Spread in the two cake tins, dividing it equally, and place in the preheated oven to bake until the cakes test done in the centers, or for about 40 minutes. Turn out onto cake racks to cool thoroughly, before frosting with Mocha-Cocoa Frosting.

MOCHA-COCOA FROSTING

⅓ *cup sweet butter*
4 *cups confectioner's sugar*
½ *teaspoon salt*
4 *tablespoons cocoa*
⅓ *cup clear, very strong black coffee*
1 *teaspoon vanilla*

Cream the sweet butter until very smooth and soft. Sift together the confectioner's sugar, salt, and cocoa. Add the mixture gradually to the butter. Stir in the coffee until the frosting is the right consistency to spread. Flavor with vanilla, and spread between the two layers of cake, and over the top and sides of the cake.

BUTTERMILK CHOCOLATE CAKE
(SERVES 6)

Preheat oven to 350°

2 *squares (2 ounces) unsweetened chocolate*
1 *cup flour*
1 *cup granulated sugar*
¼ *teaspoon baking powder*
½ *teaspoon baking soda*
½ *teaspoon salt*
¼ *cup soft butter*
½ *cup cold water*
½ *teaspoon vanilla*

1 *egg, unbeaten*
⅓ *cup buttermilk*

Butter copiously and flour lightly an 8-inch-square cake pan, 2 inches deep. Melt the chocolate in the top part of a small double boiler over hot, not boiling, water. Stir until completely melted, then set aside to cool. Put the flour, sugar, baking powder, baking soda, and salt into the smaller bowl of your electric mixer and stir well with a spoon. Add the soft butter, water, and vanilla and beat 2 minutes at medium speed, scraping the bowl often with a rubber spatula. Turn off the power and add the egg, cooled chocolate, and buttermilk, then beat 2 minutes longer, scraping the bowl frequently. Spread evenly in the cake pan and bake in the preheated oven about 40 minutes, or until the cake is shrinking away from the sides of the pan and tests done in the center. Turn out onto a cake rack to cool. When the cake is cool, cover with your favorite icing, cut in squares, and serve.

WACKY CAKE
(SERVES 6)

Preheat oven to 350°

1 *cup granulated sugar*
1½ *cups flour*
3 *tablespoons cocoa or finely grated sweet chocolate*
1 *teaspoon baking soda*
½ *teaspoon salt*
6 *tablespoons salad oil or olive oil*
1 *tablespoon cider vinegar*
1 *teaspoon vanilla*
1 *cup cold water*

    1 tablespoon confectioner's sugar (optional)
    1 cup heavy cream, whipped slightly

Sift sugar, flour, cocoa, soda, and salt into an ungreased round cake tin. Make 6 wells in the dry ingredients, using the back of a large tablespoon. Mix together the oil, vinegar, and vanilla, stir, and pour into the holes, distributing the mixture equally. Pour over all the cold water and stir and beat well with a large silver fork until the mixture is smooth and free from lumps. Place in the preheated oven and bake until the cake tests done in the center, or for about 35 to 40 minutes. Serve right from the pan while still warm, cut in pie-shaped pieces. Sprinkle the top with confectioner's sugar, if you like, and top with slightly whipped heavy cream.

KATHERINE'S LITHUANIAN SWEET BREAD
(2 LARGE LOAVES)
    1 cup seedless raisins (washed and dried)
    1 pint scalded milk
    ½ cup (1 bar) salted butter
    ½ teaspoon salt
    1 cup granulated sugar
    Grated rind of 1 lemon
    1 yeast cake
    ¼ cup warm water
    About 8 cups all-purpose flour
    3 eggs, well beaten

Butter copiously 2 bread pans, 10 inches by 4½ inches by 3 inches. Wash and dry the raisins. Scald the milk in a 2-quart enamel pan, add the butter, salt, sugar, and lemon rind. Cool to lukewarm. Dissolve the yeast in ¼ cup warm water, and stir it into the milk mixture. Gradually add 2 cups flour, sifting it in. Beat with a rotary beater until the mixture is smooth and free from lumps. Cover and set aside in a warm place to double in bulk.

Place in a large mixing bowl and add the well-beaten eggs. Stir and gradually add sufficient additional flour to make a dough that doesn't stick to the bowl, or about 6 additional cups. Before adding the last cup of flour add the raisins and continue mixing with your hands, kneading it well. Place the dough in the two well-buttered bread tins, packing it in smoothly and evenly. Cover with buttered waxed paper, and a dish towel wrung out in hot water. Set to rise in a warm spot until doubled in size, or for about 2¼ hours.

Preheat the oven to 350°–375°. Remove the cloth and waxed paper and place the loaves in the oven, on the center shelf, to bake. Reduce the heat to 325° after about 20 minutes, and continue baking until the loaves test done and are a golden brown, or for about 1 hour in all. Turn out at once onto a cake rack to cool.

SPICE CUPCAKES
(3 DOZEN CUPCAKES)
Preheat oven to 300°–325°

> ½ *pound* (1½ *cups*) *seedless raisins, lightly floured*
> ½ *cup soft butter*
> 1 *cup granulated sugar*
> 1 *cup molasses*
> ½ *cup buttermilk*
> 3 *eggs, unbeaten*
> 2½ *cups flour*

2 *teaspoons baking powder*
1 *teaspoon cinnamon*
1 *teaspoon nutmeg*
½ *teaspoon cloves*
1 *teaspoon vanilla*

Butter copiously 3 dozen muffin tins. Wash the raisins in warm water, dry well on paper toweling, and flour lightly. Cream the butter with the sugar, and stir in the molasses and buttermilk. Beat the eggs one at a time. Sift the flour, baking powder, and spices together, then add gradually to the first ingredients, and stir in the vanilla. Last of all, fold in the raisins. Spoon the mixture into the muffin tins, place in a slow oven, and bake until they test done, or for about 20 to 25 minutes. Serve while still warm, or reheat if necessary.

JELLY ROLL
(SERVES 6–8)

Preheat oven to 325°

¾ *cup sifted granulated sugar*
¾ *cup sifted cake flour*
1½ *tablespoons cornstarch*
1¼ *teaspoons baking powder*
4 *eggs at room temperature, separated*
Pinch of salt
3 *tablespoons cold water*
1 *tablespoon strained lemon juice*
½ *teaspoon lemon extract*
Extra superfine sugar
Jam or jelly

Butter the sides and bottom of a jelly-roll pan (cookie sheet with sides). Line it neatly with white shelfpaper and butter the paper well.

Sift some granulated sugar and measure out ¾ cup of it. Sift some flour and measure out ¾ cup of it, then add the cornstarch and baking powder to the flour and sift again. Separate the yolks from the whites of the eggs. Add the pinch of salt to the egg whites and beat until stiff but not dry, then beat in gradually ¼ cup of the sifted granulated sugar. With the same beater, beat together the yolks, water, lemon juice, and lemon extract. Continue beating until the mixture is lemon-colored, then beat in gradually the remaining ½ cup sugar. Continue beating until very stiff. Fold in the whites and, last of all, the sifted flour. Do not beat after adding the egg whites. Spread evenly in the paper-lined pan, and bake in the preheated oven until the cake is a delicate brown, or for about 18 minutes.

In the meantime, dampen a dish towel and cover it with a sheet of heavy waxed paper. Sprinkle the paper with a thin coating of superfine sugar. When the cake is done, turn it out onto the sugared paper and quickly pull off the buttered paper. Cut away thin strips from the outer sides and ends of the cake. Spread the cake with a cup or more of your favorite jam or jelly, beaten until soft. Roll up the cake, placed horizontally in front of you, and wrap securely in a dry cloth or heavy waxed paper, until serving time. Cut in thick slices, and serve with it a Lemon and Vanilla Sauce (see page 128).

SCRIPTURE CAKE
(SERVES 8–10)

Preheat oven to 350°

Judges 5:25 (½ cup butter) at room temperature

Jeremiah 6:20 (*1 cup sugar*)
Isaiah 10:14 (*4 eggs, separated*)
Exodus 16:31 (*1 tablespoon honey*)
I Kings 4:22 (*2 cups flour*)
Leviticus 2:13 (*½ teaspoon salt*)
I Corinthians 5:6 (*2 teaspoons baking powder*)
I Kings 10:10 (*¾ teaspoon ground cinnamon*)
　　　　　　(*¼ teaspoon ground cloves*)
　　　　　　(*¼ teaspoon allspice*)
　　　　　　(*¼ teaspoon nutmeg*)
Judges 4:19 (*⅓ cup milk*)
Genesis 43:11 (*½ cup finely slivered blanched almonds*)
I Samuel 30:12 (*¾ cup chopped dried figs [7 of them]*)
I Samuel 30:12 (*¾ cup seeded raisins, soaked 5 minutes in warm
　　water, then well dried on paper toweling*)
　　　　　　(*½ teaspoon vanilla*)
　　　　　　(*½ teaspoon almond extract*)

Copiously butter one bread pan 8 by 4 by 3 inches and two small loaf pans 4½ by 2¾ by 2 inches. Line the bottoms and sides with heavy waxed paper.

　Cream the butter and gradually add the sugar, beating until light. Add the egg yolks, one at a time, beating thoroughly after each addition. Beat in the honey. Sift together the dry ingredients and add alternately with the milk and beat only until smooth. Add the vanilla and almond extract and stir in the nuts, figs, and raisins, lightly floured. Beat the egg whites until stiff, and fold them in. Pour into the prepared large and small loaf pans.

Bake in the preheated oven for 35 or 40 minutes, at which time remove the small loaves and continue baking the large one until it tests done in the center, or for about 1 hour in all.

Cool the cakes in the pans for 5 minutes before turning them out onto a cake rack. Peel off the paper and turn the cakes right side up to cool.

HELEN'S RHUBARB SHORTCAKE
(SERVES 6–8)

Preheat oven to 450°

> *About 2 pounds firm, young pink rhubarb*
> *About 1½ cups granulated sugar plus 3 tablespoons*
> *3 cups flour*
> *6 teaspoons baking powder*
> *¾ teaspoon salt*
> *6 tablespoons butter*
> *1¼ cups milk*
> *2 tablespoons soft butter*
> *2 cups heavy cream, whipped*

Remove the leaves and root ends from the rhubarb. Wash and cut in 1-inch pieces. Place in the top part of a large (2-quart) enamel double boiler over boiling water. Cover and cook for ½ hour, stirring occasionally. By this time it will have made its own juice. Place on direct heat and boil 5 minutes, being careful that it doesn't stick, then sweeten to taste with about 1½ cups sugar. Stir and simmer another 5 minutes. Remove from the fire, cool, and chill until you are ready to use.

In the meantime butter well a 9-inch layer-cake tin. Sift the flour, baking powder, salt, and 3 tablespoons sugar into a bowl. Work in the 6 tablespoons butter with a pastry cutter or your fingertips and moisten with the milk to form a soft dough. Toss out onto a floured board and knead lightly, and spread out on the buttered cake tin. Place in the preheated oven and bake until a light golden brown, or for 12 to 15 minutes. Split while hot and spread the bottom half with the soft butter. Cover with part of the chilled rhubarb and with plenty of whipped cream. Cover with the top half and spread plenty more of the rhubarb over the top. Spread over all the rest of the whipped cream and serve at once.

LEMON CAKE PIE
(2 PIES; SERVES 8–10)

Preheat oven to 450°

> 2½ cups pastry flour
> ½ teaspoon salt
> 6 tablespoons butter
> 6 tablespoons vegetable shortening
> 5 or 6 tablespoons ice water

Sift the flour and salt together and work in the shortenings, using your fingertips or a pastry blender. Moisten with ice water, form into two flat balls, wrap in waxed paper, and chill for half an hour. Then roll out and line 2 large pie plates, trim the edges, and crimp.

FOR THE FILLING

> 5 large eggs, separated
> 2 cups granulated sugar
> 2 tablespoons butter, melted
> 4 tablespoons flour
> Grated rind and strained juice of 2 lemons
> 2 cups milk

Beat the egg whites until stiff with a rotary beater and set aside.

Using the same beater, beat the yolks until light and creamy, then gradually beat in the sugar. Stir in the melted butter, flour, and grated rind and juice of the lemons. Then add the milk, and beat again until thoroughly mixed. Now fold the whites in carefully and pour the mixture into the unbaked pie shells. Bake 10 minutes in the preheated oven, turn the heat down to 350°, and bake about 45 to 50 minutes longer. If the tops should start to brown too much, make covers of foil and set over the pies. Serve cold but not chilled.

BLUEBERRY TEA MUFFINS
(12 MUFFINS)
Preheat oven to 350°–375°

> 1 *cup large blueberries*
> ¼ *cup sweet butter*
> ¾ *cup granulated sugar*
> 1 *egg, well beaten*
> 1½ *cups all-purpose flour*
> ¾ *teaspoon salt*
> 2 *teaspoons baking powder*
> ½ *cup milk*
> ½ *teaspoon vanilla*
> *Grated rind of ½ lemon*

Pick over the blueberries, wash, and dry well on paper toweling. Cream together the butter and sugar. Add the egg and beat until light. Sift together the flour, salt, and baking powder, return to the sifter, and add gradually to the first mixture, alternately with the milk. Flavor with vanilla and lemon rind, and fold in the blueberries, using a large fork so as not to crush the berries.

Place in well-buttered muffin tins and bake until the muffins are a light golden brown or for about 35 minutes. Serve hot.

STONEHOUSE INN HOT-MILK CUPCAKES
(15 CUPCAKES)

Preheat oven to 350°

> 1 *cup flour*
> 1½ *teaspoons baking powder*
> *Pinch of salt*
> ½ *cup milk*
> 1 *tablespoon butter*
> 2 *eggs*
> 1 *cup granulated sugar*
> 1 *teaspoon vanilla*
> ½ *teaspoon lemon extract*

Butter and flour 15 cupcake tins. Sift together the flour, baking powder, and salt. Heat together ½ cup milk and 1 tablespoon butter. Beat the eggs and beat the sugar in gradually. Add the vanilla and lemon extract. Fold in the sifted flour. Last of all, add the hot milk gradually. When the batter is well mixed, fill the tins and bake in the preheated oven for about 20 minutes. Turn out on a cake rack to cool. Frost if desired.

NINE

Pies, Tarts, & Cookies

MY PIE CRUST
(2 SMALL CRUSTS)
Preheat oven to 400°–450°

      2½ cups pastry or all-purpose flour
      1 teaspoon salt
      6 tablespoons vegetable shortening
      6 tablespoons butter
      3 to 6 tablespoons ice water

Sift the flour and salt into a bowl and work the butter and vegetable shortening into it with your fingertips. When mealy in
consistency, moisten with ice water, adding a small amount at a
time. Form into 2 balls, one slightly larger than the other.

For the under crust, use the smaller ball. Roll out to about ⅛-
inch thickness, keeping the dough in a circular shape. To lift
into the pan, place the rolling pin crosswise at the top of the
circle, lift the top of the pastry, and hold it against the pin. Then

roll the pin toward you, rolling the pastry up onto the pin as you go. Unroll onto the pan so the pastry completely covers the pan. Let it settle well down into the pan before you trim off the excess pastry with floured scissors, leaving, however, about ½ inch hanging over the edge.

Fill the pie with whatever filling it is to have, then roll the second half of the pastry in the same manner, making a slightly larger circle. Moisten the rim of the lower crust, then roll up the pastry for the top onto the pin, unroll it over the filled crust, and with scissors cut off at the same point as the under crust. Press the edges together, and roll under—so as to make a thick edge—then with fingers or fork crimp the edges together. Prick the entire top with a floured fork, or make several slashes in the top, before baking. Place in the preheated oven for 10 minutes, then reduce the heat to 350° and continue baking until the filling is cooked and the pie is well browned all over. The time required will depend on the filling used.

For a 1-crust pie, simply use half the recipe.

GRANDMA PARKER'S PIE CRUST
(3 SMALL CRUSTS OR 2 LARGER)
3 cups sifted all-purpose flour
½ teaspoon baking powder
¼ teaspoon salt
⅓ cup butter
⅔ cup lard
5 or 6 tablespoons ice water

Sift together the flour, baking powder, and salt. Add the butter and lard and chop with a pastry blender until in very fine crumbs. Moisten with just enough ice water to make a dough that holds together. Roll in waxed paper and refrigerate a short while before rolling out, on a lightly floured pastry cloth or board, to the desired sizes.

ALMOND CREAM PIE
(SERVES 6)

Preheat oven to 350°
> *1 unbaked pie crust (see page 169)*
> *¼ pound (1 heaping cup) blanched slivered almonds*
> *1 teaspoon rosewater*
> *Pinch of salt*
> *¼ teaspoon almond extract*
> *1 cup light cream*
> *6 egg yolks*
> *1 cup granulated sugar*

Line a 9-inch pie plate with pie crust and crimp the edges. Chill. Put the slivered almonds in an electric blender. Add the rosewater, salt, and almond extract, and run while you count 5. Add ¼ cup cream and run the blender while you count 20. Add another ¼ cup of cream and blend, counting 10, add the egg yolks, and blend, counting 10, then stir in the remaining ½ cup cream. Last of all stir in the sugar. Run the blender again while you count 20. Pour the mixture into the chilled pastry-lined pie shell and bake in the preheated oven until the pie is a golden brown all over and it tests done in the center, or for about 45 minutes. Serve partially cooled.

SUGAR PIE
(SERVES 8—2 PIES)

Preheat oven to 450°

> *Pastry for a 1-crust pie (page 169)*
> 1 *cup lumpy light- or dark-brown sugar*
> 4 *tablespoons butter*
> 1 *teaspoon cinnamon*
> ½ *cup light cream*

Mix the pastry, chill in the refrigerator for about 15 minutes, divide the dough in half and line 2 pie plates. Crimp the edges. Sprinkle half the sugar over each, leaving it lumpy, so that the crust shows through in spots. Sprinkle the cinnamon over each, then trickle ¼ cup of cream over the sugar in each crust. Bake in the preheated oven until the filling is bubbling hot and the crust is lightly browned, or for about 18 minutes in all. Cut in pie-shaped pieces and serve when slightly cooled.

BLUEBERRY TART
(SERVES 6)

Preheat oven to 350°–375°

> 2 *tablespoons butter*
> 1 *cup light-brown sugar*
> 1 *cup granulated sugar*
> ½ *teaspoon salt*
> ¼ *cup flour*
> 2 *tablespoons strained lemon juice*
> 1 *quart dry frozen blueberries*

Pastry for a 1-crust pie (page 169)
1 cup heavy cream (whipped until almost stiff)

Roll out and line a 10-inch pie plate with pastry.

Place the butter, brown sugar, granulated sugar, salt, flour, and lemon juice in a heavy saucepan. Add half the frozen berries, place on a very low flame, and stir constantly with a wooden spoon until the berries join their juice and collapse a bit. When it all comes to a boil and has thickened a bit (about 5 minutes in all), remove from the fire and add the remainder of the frozen berries. Stir to combine the cooked and uncooked berries. Cool and refrigerate until ready to use.

Crimp the edges of the pie crust, prick the bottom in a few places with prongs of a fork, and bake until a golden brown, or for about 15 to 20 minutes. Cool, and when ready to serve, fill with the chilled blueberries. Cover the blueberries with the whipped cream and serve at once.

HURRY-UP BLUEBERRY TART
(SERVES 6)

Preheat oven to 450°

1 nine-inch frozen, ready-to-bake crust
1 quart large blueberries, picked over, washed, and drained
1 cup commercial or homemade Blueberry Jam (page 220)
½ pint heavy cream, whipped or plain (optional)

Place the frozen crust in its foil tin in an oven-proof pie plate of the same size. This is to reinforce the tart. Bake, following the directions on the package. Cool partially and fill heaping full with the well-drained fresh berries. Pour the blueberry jam over the berries and serve soon thereafter with or without cream.

BANBURY TARTS
(12 TARTS)

Pastry for a 2-crust pie (page 169), chilled
1 *cup shelled English walnuts*
1 *cup white seedless raisins*
Grated rind and strained juice of 1 large lemon
1 *cup granulated sugar*
1 *tablespoon boiling water*
1 *tablespoon butter*
1 *egg*
1 *teaspoon vanilla*
2 *tablespoons cracker crumbs*
Milk
Confectioner's sugar in which you have kept a vanilla bean

Chop the nuts fine in a wooden bowl and add the raisins, likewise chopped fairly fine. Put the two in a bowl and add the grated rind and lemon juice. Stir in the sugar and moisten with the boiling water in which you have melted the butter. Beat the egg lightly and stir it into the rest and flavor with vanilla. Sprinkle the whole with cracker crumbs and stir well.

Now butter 2 large cookie sheets and preheat the oven to 450°. Roll out the chilled pastry until ⅛ inch thick, then cut it carefully into 4-inch squares. Separate one from the other slightly and place a scant tablespoon of filling on each. Dip your fingers in cold water and moisten the edges of each square. Then fold them over to form triangles and press the edges firmly. Last of all, dip a fork in flour and crimp the cut edges of each. Lay them on the cookie sheets and prick each one 3 times with a fork. Refrigerate for 15 minutes. When the tarts are chilled, paint each one with a little milk and bake in the preheated oven for 20 to 25 minutes until lightly browned. Serve while still warm if possible. If not, reheat them slightly. Just before serving, sprinkle lightly with confectioner's sugar in which you have kept a vanilla bean.

GREEN-TOMATO PIE
(SERVES 6)

Preheat oven to 400°

> *Pastry for a 2-crust pie (page 169)*
> *5 large green tomatoes*
> *1 generous cup granulated sugar*
> *½ cup cider vinegar*
> *¼ teaspoon ground allspice*
> *¼ teaspoon ground cinnamon*
> *2 teaspoons flour*
> *2 tablespoons butter*

Have ready a pie tin lined with pastry. Wash the tomatoes, remove the green cores, and slice paper-thin. Sprinkle immediately with the sugar and vinegar. Add the spices to the flour and mix into the tomato mixture. Place in the bottom crust and dot with the butter. Cover with the second crust and roll the edges under securely. Crimp prettily with your fingertips. Make a 1-inch crisscross incision in the center of the crust and insert into the hole a rosette made of a strip of pastry wrapped around your forefinger. This is to allow the steam to escape. Place the pie in the preheated oven and bake until a golden brown all over, or for about 50 to 60 minutes, decreasing the heat slightly if necessary at the end of the cooking time.

RICH SQUASH PIE
(SERVES 6)

Preheat oven to 450°

> *Pastry for a 1-crust pie (page 169)*
> *Slightly beaten white of 1 egg*
> *3 eggs, slightly beaten*
> *1 cup canned squash*
> *1 cup granulated sugar*
> *¾ teaspoon salt*
> *1 teaspoon cinnamon*
> *½ teaspoon nutmeg*
> *¾ teaspoon ginger*
> *1 cup heavy cream*

Line a 9-inch pie plate with plain pastry and crimp the edges. Paint the bottom of the crust with the slightly beaten egg white. Add the beaten eggs to the squash, stir in the sugar, salt, and spices, mix well, and stir in the cream. Place in the crust and bake for 10 minutes on the lower shelf of the preheated oven, transfer to the middle shelf, reduce the heat to moderate (350°–375°), and bake until the pie tests done in the center, or for about 40 minutes longer.

MAGGIE'S RAISIN PIE
(SERVES 6)

Preheat oven to 425°

> *1 cup seeded raisins put through a food chopper*
> *1 cup shelled English walnuts put through same chopper*
> *½ cup fresh butter, well creamed*

¼ *teaspoon salt*
¾ *cup granulated sugar*
3 *eggs*
1 *teaspoon vanilla*
Pastry for a 2-crust pie (page 169)
½ *pint heavy cream*

Prepare the raisins and walnuts, putting them through the food chopper in the order given. Cream the butter, salt, and sugar thoroughly in a bowl. Add the eggs one at a time, beating well after each egg. Blend in the raisins and nuts. Flavor with the vanilla.

Place in the pie shell, spreading the mixture evenly, and cover with lattice strips. Bake in the preheated hot oven for 10 minutes. Reduce the heat to 325° and bake about 30 to 35 minutes longer. Serve warm with or without cream.

APPLE CUSTARD PIE
(SERVES 6)

Preheat oven to 450°

> *Pastry for a 1-crust pie (page 169)*
> 3 *eggs, beaten*
> 1 *cup applesauce*
> 1 *cup rich milk*
> *Pinch of salt*
> ½ *cup granulated sugar*
> 1 *teaspoon vanilla*

First line the pie plate with homemade pastry, or substitute 1 frozen crust. Keep cold while you mix the filling.

Mix together the beaten eggs, applesauce, milk, salt, and

sugar, and stir in the vanilla. Pour the mixture into the chilled crust, and bake in the preheated oven for 10 minutes, then reduce the heat to 350° and continue baking until the pie tests done in the center, or for about 30 to 35 minutes. Serve lukewarm.

CHERRY PIE
(SERVES 6)

Preheat oven to 450°

> Pastry for a 2-crust pie (see page 169)
> ½ teaspoon almond extract
> 1 can (1 pound 5 ounces) cherry pie filling
> Small quantity of light cream
> Pitcher of heavy cream if desired

Line an 8- or 9-inch pie plate with plain pastry. Add the almond extract to the cherry pie filling, stir, and pour into the lined pan. Cover with the second circle of pastry, trim the edges, roll under (follow directions on page 169) and crimp. Roll out the scraps and cut three strips 1½ inches wide, then cut again so as to form six equal-sized diamond-shaped pieces. Make an incision in the center of the pie. Roll out another strip of pastry and roll it up around your forefinger so as to form a rosette. Paint the surface of the pie with light cream, using a pastry brush. Lay the six diamond-shaped pieces around the incision, forming a star, paint these with more cream, then insert the rosette (which you have dipped into cream) well down into the center of the pie, to make a vent for the steam to escape while the pie is baking. With a knife make five more incisions around the star. Place in the preheated oven and bake about 30 to 35 minutes or until the crust is a golden brown. Serve while still warm, with or without heavy cream.

HELEN BUDD'S CHOCOLATE MERINGUE PIE
(SERVES 6–8)

Preheat oven to 450°

½ *cup* (1½ *ounces or* 1½ *squares*) *grated unsweetened chocolate*

1 *cup hot water*

3 *tablespoons butter*

1 *tablespoon vanilla*

1 *cup sugar*

3 *egg yolks, well beaten*

2 *tablespoons cornstarch dissolved in 2 tablespoons cold water*

1 *pie crust baked 15–18 minutes in a 450° oven (page 169)*

Put the grated chocolate in the top part of an enamel double boiler. Add the hot water, butter, vanilla, sugar, and well-beaten egg yolks. Stir well and add the dissolved cornstarch. Place over boiling water and cook, stirring constantly, until well thickened, or for about 8 minutes. Cool thoroughly, stirring occasionally, before filling the baked crust.

FOR THE MERINGUE

Preheat oven to 350°

> ¾ *teaspoon cream of tartar*
> 3 *egg whites*
> 6 *tablespoons granulated sugar*
> 1 *teaspoon vanilla*

Add the cream of tartar to the egg whites and beat until they are stiff enough to hold a peak, then gradually beat in the sugar, flavor with the vanilla, and continue beating until very stiff. Pile lightly on the chocolate filling, being sure the meringue touches the crust all around, to prevent its shrinking away from the edge while browning. Bake until the meringue is a golden brown all over, or for about 10 to 12 minutes. Serve cold but not chilled.

VINEGAR PIE
(SERVES 6)

Preheat oven to 450°

        Plain pastry for a 1-crust pie (page 169)
        ¼ cup cider vinegar
        ¾ cup water
        2 tablespoons butter
        1½ cups granulated sugar
        5 tablespoons cornstarch
        2 egg yolks
        1 teaspoon lemon extract

Line a 9-inch pie plate with plain pastry, prick the bottom all over with a fork, and bake until the pastry is a light golden brown, or for about 15 minutes. Heat the vinegar, water, and butter together in the top part of an enamel double boiler. Cool slightly while you sift together the sugar and cornstarch. Beat the egg yolks and gradually stir in the liquid mixture. Stir this into the sugar-and-cornstarch mixture and flavor with lemon extract. Place over boiling water, and stir constantly with a wooden spoon until the mixture is well thickened, or for about 15 to 20 minutes. Cool completely before pouring into the baked crust. Serve shortly thereafter.

BOSTON CREAM PIE
(SERVES 6)

A friend tells me that in her Massachusetts home this dish was called "Pudding-Cake-Pie" because it combines elements of all. Preheat oven to 350°–375°

FOR THE CAKE

> 2 *cups sifted cake flour*
> 3 *teaspoons baking powder*
> ¼ *teaspoon salt*
> 4 *tablespoons* (½ *bar*) *butter at room temperature*
> 1 *cup granulated sugar*
> 1 *egg*
> ¾ *cup milk*
> 1 *teaspoon vanilla*
> *Confectioner's sugar*

Butter copiously two round 8-inch layer-cake tins and dust lightly with flour. Sift together three times the flour, baking powder, and salt. Cream the butter and gradually add the granulated sugar. When the mixture is light and fluffy, add the unbeaten egg and beat well. Add the flour alternately with the milk, beating well after each addition. Add the vanilla and place in the cake tins, dividing the batter equally. Bake in the preheated oven for about 25 to 30 minutes, or until the cake is lightly browned on top. Turn out onto cake racks to cool.

FOR THE FILLING

> ½ *cup all-purpose flour*
> ½ *cup granulated sugar*
> ¼ *teaspoon salt*
> 2 *whole eggs*

> 2 *cups milk, scalded*
> 1½ *tablespoons butter*
> 1 *teaspoon vanilla*

In the meantime make the filling. Mix together the flour, sugar, and salt. Beat the eggs lightly and stir into the dry ingredients. Add slowly, stirring constantly, the scalded milk, making a smooth paste. Cook over boiling water, stirring constantly, until the mixture is smooth and thick, or for about 5 minutes, then continue cooking for another 5 minutes. Remove from the heat and cool partially before stirring in the butter. Add the vanilla and allow the mixture to stand until cold, stirring occasionally.

Split the 2 cake layers, making 4, and put them together with the custard filling on a large round dessert platter. Sprinkle copiously with confectioner's sugar and serve cut in six generous wedge-shaped pieces.

CRANBERRY-RAISIN PIE
(SERVES 6)

Preheat oven to 450°

> *Recipe for a 2-crust pie (page 169)*
> 1 *cup cranberries, washed and cut in half*
> 1 *cup seedless raisins, washed and dried*
> ¾ *cup granulated sugar*
> *Pinch of salt*
> 2 *tablespoons flour*
> 1 *tablespoon butter*
> 1 *cup heavy cream*

Roll out half the pastry and line an 8- or 9-inch pie plate. Mix the cranberries and raisins with the sugar, salt, and flour, and turn into the pastry-lined plate. Moisten the edge of the crust with water. Roll out the remainder of the pastry. Dot the berries with the butter, cover with the pastry, press the edges together, and roll under, making a firm rim. Crimp prettily and make several slashes in the top crust. Bake 10 minutes in the preheated oven, reduce the heat to 350° and continue cooking about 30 minutes longer. Serve warm with heavy cream.

ALMOND CAKES
(20 COOKIES)

Preheat oven to 300°

> ½ *cup butter, at room temperature*
> *1 cup powdered sugar*
> *1 cup flour*
> ⅓ *cup milk*
> *1 teaspoon almond extract*
> *1 package (3-ounce) blanched sliced almonds*

Cream together the butter and sugar. Add the flour and milk alternately, making a smooth batter. Add the almond extract, and with the help of a large spatula spread the mixture evenly over a well-buttered cookie sheet. Sprinkle the almonds evenly over the batter. Place in the preheated oven and bake until the surface is a golden brown all over, or for about 35 minutes. Remove from the oven and cut into 20 squares. Loosen with a small spatula while still hot, but do not remove from the pan until cool.

THICK OR THIN GINGER COOKIES
(6 DOZEN OR MORE)

These cookies are fun to make and are delicious, made either wafer-thin or thick, rolled out and cut in desired shapes, or just dropped by teaspoonfuls onto lightly buttered cookie sheets, plain or enhanced with raisins and/or candied ginger. I suggest you make some of each as follows:

Preheat oven to 350°–375°

> ⅔ *cup soft salted butter*
>
> ½ *cup granulated sugar*
>
> 1 *egg, well beaten*
>
> 1 *cup light molasses*
>
> 1 *tablespoon cider vinegar*
>
> 2 *tablespoons cold water*
>
> 4½ *cups sifted all-purpose flour*
>
> 1 *tablespoon powdered ginger*
>
> 1 *tablespoon baking soda*
>
> ½ *cup seedless golden raisins* (*optional*)
>
> 2 *tablespoons finely cut candied ginger* (*optional*)
>
> *Extra granulated sugar*

Cream the butter with the sugar until light and fluffy. Add the beaten egg and mix well, then stir in the molasses, vinegar, and cold water. Sift some all-purpose flour and measure out 4½ cups of it. Place in the sifter again, and add to it the ginger and baking soda. Sift once, then again, adding the flour mixture gradually to the first ingredients. This will make a fairly stiff dough.

Wrap ⅓ of it in waxed paper, and place in the freezing compartment of the refrigerator to chill for about 30 minutes, while you use ½ the remaining dough to make plain drop cookies. Using a teaspoon, drop the dough onto lightly buttered cookie sheets, not too close together, and bake 12 to 14 minutes in the preheated oven. When done, loosen with a small spatula and transfer to cookie racks to cool. Now add either the candied ginger or the raisins or both to the remaining unchilled dough and make and bake in the same manner as the plain drop cookies. When they are done, transfer to cookie racks to cool.

By this time, the chilled dough should be just right to roll out, thick or thin, on a well-floured pastry cloth or board. Cut into desired shapes with cookie cutters, place on lightly buttered cookie sheets, and bake 12 to 14 minutes. Loosen immediately with a small spatula and transfer to cookie racks to cool. If you have made these thick, a little granulated sugar may be sprinkled over the cookies before baking, but the thin ones are best just plain.

This should make about 2 dozen plain drop cookies, about the same number of the fruit ones, and 2 dozen or more rolled-out-and-cut cookies, depending on how big or how thick they are.

NANTUCKET GINGER COOKIES
(2½ DOZEN)
Preheat oven to 350°

> ½ cup (1 bar) butter
> ⅔ cup light-brown sugar
> ⅓ cup molasses
> ⅓ cup water
> 2 scant cups flour
> 1 teaspoon baking soda
> 1 teaspoon powdered ginger

Cream the butter and sugar together; stir in the molasses and water. Sift together the flour, soda, and ginger. Sift again into the first mixture. Drop by heaping teaspoonfuls onto well-buttered cookie sheets. Bake 11 or 12 minutes in the preheated oven. Loosen immediately from the pan, using a spatula, but wait until the cookies have slightly cooled before transferring them to a cookie rack. Store, when cold, in a tightly covered container.

RICH BROWN-EDGE COOKIES
(ABOUT 30 COOKIES)

Preheat oven to 350°

> ½ cup butter, at room temperature
> ⅓ cup granulated sugar
> 1 egg, well beaten
> ¾ cup sifted all-purpose flour
> 1 teaspoon vanilla

Cream the soft butter and sugar together until light and fluffy, add the well-beaten egg, beat again until light and smooth, then gradually stir in the sifted flour. Flavor with the vanilla. Drop by teaspoonfuls at least 2 inches apart onto 2 buttered cookie sheets. Bake in the preheated oven until the cookies are lightly browned around the edges—for 12 to 15 minutes. Remove at once with a spatula and place on racks to cool.

SUSIE'S LACE COOKIES
(3 DOZEN OR MORE)

Preheat oven to 350°

> 1 cup butter, at room temperature
> 1 cup granulated sugar

½ *cup light-brown sugar*
2 *cups Quick Quaker Oats*
1 *teaspoon vanilla*

Cream the butter, add the two sugars gradually, then add the oats and vanilla. Drop by teaspoonfuls onto unbuttered cookie sheets, keeping them quite far apart, as they spread out while baking and should not touch each other. Place in the preheated oven and bake about 10 minutes. Remove from the oven and allow the cookies to cool 5 minutes before removing them carefully from the pan, using a spatula. Store in air-tight cookie tins.

DAINTIES
(3½ DOZEN)

Preheat oven to 350°

2 *eggs*
1 *cup light-brown sugar, well packed*
¾ *cup all-purpose flour*
½ *teaspoon salt*
¼ *teaspoon baking soda*
¼ *teaspoon cream of tartar*
1 *teaspoon vanilla*
¼ *teaspoon almond extract*
1½ *cups (6 ounces) finely chopped pecans*

Beat the eggs well and gradually beat in the brown sugar. Sift together the flour, salt, soda, and cream of tartar, and blend with the eggs and sugar. Stir in the flavorings and chopped nuts. Drop from a teaspoon onto well-buttered cookie sheets. Bake 12 to 15 minutes or until cookies are a golden brown. Remove immediately from the cookie sheets with a pancake turner and allow to cool on cookie racks.

PEANUT-BUTTER COOKIES
(ABOUT 40 COOKIES)

Preheat oven to 375°

> ¼ *cup butter, at room temperature*
> ½ *cup peanut butter, at room temperature*
> 1 *egg*
> ½ *cup granulated light-brown sugar*
> ½ *cup granulated sugar*
> 1 *teaspoon vanilla*
> 1 *cup flour*
> 1 *teaspoon baking soda*
> 20 *pecan halves or blanched almonds (optional)*

Cream the butter and peanut butter together until well mixed, then add the egg and continue beating until very light. Gradually add the two sugars, sifted together, and flavor with the vanilla. Sift the flour with the baking soda once, then again, adding it gradually to the other ingredients. Shape into 1-inch balls, using your hands, and place on two lightly buttered cookie sheets. Press into half of them a blanched almond or pecan half. Bake until the cookies are a light golden brown all over, or for about 10 minutes. Loosen from the cookie sheets while still warm. Cool on racks.

MACAROONS
(2 DOZEN)

Preheat oven to 300°–325°

> 1 *can (8-ounce) pure almond paste, at room temperature*
> 1 *cup superfine sugar*

2 *egg whites, unbeaten*
½ *teaspoon almond extract*

Line a large cookie sheet with typewriter paper. Cut the almond paste into fine slivers with a paring knife. Place in the small bowl of an electric beater. Add the sugar and egg whites (unbeaten) and the almond extract. Mix until very smooth and free from lumps. Place the mixture in a pastry bag or, better still, a cookie press (metal variety) with a star tube. Squeeze the dough out onto the paper-lined cookie sheets in mounds about the size of a half dollar. Bake in the preheated oven for 25 to 30 minutes. Remove the cookies from the oven and cool. Turn them upside down while still attached to the paper and moisten the paper. Turn over once more and with the help of a small spatula loosen and remove the macaroons one at a time. Place on a cookie rack to dry.

TOLL HOUSE COOKIES
(ABOUT 40 COOKIES)

Preheat oven to 375°

½ *cup soft butter*
⅜ *cup brown sugar*
⅜ *cup granulated sugar*
1 *egg, well beaten*
½ *teaspoon baking soda*
½ *teaspoon hot water*
1⅛ *cup flour*
½ *teaspoon salt*
½ *cup broken walnuts or pecans*
1 *package (6 ounces) semi-sweet chocolate morsels*
½ *teaspoon vanilla*

Butter copiously 3 cookie sheets. Cream the butter in a mixing bowl with the brown sugar and the granulated sugar. Stir in the well-beaten egg. Dissolve the soda in the hot water and add it to the mixture. Add the flour sifted with the salt, and beat until smooth. Add the nuts, chocolate bits, and vanilla. Chill for half an hour, then drop by teapoonfuls onto the cookie sheets. Bake in the preheated oven for about 10 to 12 minutes. To avoid breaking the cookies, loosen them with a spatula as soon as they are baked.

SNICKERDOODLES
(ABOUT 4 DOZEN)

Preheat oven to 325°

    1 cup seedless raisins
    2 cups flour
    2 teaspoons baking powder
    ½ teaspoon salt
    1 egg, well beaten
    1 cup sifted granulated sugar
    2 tablespoons very soft, but not melted, butter
    ⅓ cup milk
    1½ teaspoons vanilla
    About 2 tablespoons cinnamon sugar

Butter copiously two large cookie sheets. Wash, dry, and cut or chop the raisins coarsely. Sift the flour, baking powder, and salt together. Beat the egg well, and stir in the sugar. When well mixed, stir in the soft butter. Add the raisins, stir, and gradually add the dry ingredients alternately with the milk. Add the vanilla and beat well. Drop by teaspoonfuls, not too close together, onto the cookie sheets. Sprinkle generously with cinnamon sugar. Bake about 20 to 25 minutes in the preheated oven. Remove from the cookie sheets with a pancake turner, and place on cake racks to cool, before storing in a cookie jar.

WALNUT COOKIES
(4 DOZEN)

Preheat oven to 350°–375°

>   2 *eggs*
>   1 *cup light-brown sugar, firmly packed*
>   ¾ *cup flour*
>   ¼ *teaspoon cream of tartar*
>   ¼ *teaspoon baking soda*
>   ½ *teaspoon salt*
>   ½ *teaspoon vanilla*
>   6 *ounces chopped English walnuts*

Beat the eggs well, gradually adding the sugar. Sift together the flour, cream of tartar, soda, and salt. Stir into the eggs and sugar. Add the vanilla and nuts and drop by teaspoonfuls onto copiously buttered cookie sheets, placing them at least 1 inch apart. Bake until the cookies are a golden brown, or for about 12 minutes. Remove from the pans immediately with a pancake turner and place on cookie racks to cool and become crisp.

MASSACHUSETTS GINGERBREAD MAN
(SERVES 6)

Preheat oven to 350°

>   ½ *cup (1 bar) butter at room temperature*
>   ½ *cup light-brown sugar, well packed*
>   1 *egg, unbeaten*

    1 *cup light molasses*
    2½ *cups all-purpose flour*
    1 *teaspoon powdered cinnamon*
    1 *teaspoon powdered ginger*
    ½ *teaspoon powdered cloves*
    ½ *teaspoon salt*
    1½ *teaspoons baking soda*
    1 *cup double-strength hot instant coffee*
Confectioner's sugar
    1 *cup or more heavy cream, beaten until almost stiff*

Cream the butter and sugar until light, add the egg, and beat with a large spoon until well mixed. Stir in the molasses. Sift the dry ingredients together once, then sift again onto the batter, and beat with the spoon until the mixture is smooth and free from lumps. Stir in the hot coffee, made of 2 teaspoons instant coffee and one cup boiling water. This will make a thin batter, which is as it should be.

    Butter copiously a large gingerbread-boy cake pan (14 inches by 7 inches) and 8 cupcake tins. Carefully fill the gingerbread-boy mold almost full, using about 4 cups batter, and place the remainder in the cupcake tins. Place all in the preheated oven and bake until the cupcakes test done in the center, or for about 30 minutes. Remove from the oven and continue cooking the gingerbread boy until it tests done too, or for 5 to 10 minutes longer. Turn all out on cake racks to cool until you are ready to serve; then reheat for a few minutes. Lift the gingerbread boy onto a large serving platter, sprinkle him with confectioner's sugar, and serve at the table with plenty of whipped cream.

PECAN BALLS
(2½ DOZEN)

Preheat oven to 300°

> 1 *cup shelled pecans, chopped fine*
> ¼ *pound butter, at room temperature*
> 2 *tablespoons granulated sugar*
> 1 *cup all-purpose flour*
> 1 *teaspoon vanilla*
> ¼ *cup confectioner's sugar*

Place nut meats in an electric blender and run while you count 5, or chop fine in a wooden bowl. Cream the butter and granulated sugar, add the flour, nuts, and vanilla. Mix well together. Shape the dough with your hands into balls, making them as round and smooth as possible. Spread out on a flat cookie sheet about 2 inches apart, and bake slowly in the preheated oven for about 40 minutes. Remove from the oven and allow to cool for at least 30 minutes. Roll in confectioner's sugar, coating them all over.

TEN

Breads, Rolls, & Muffins

ANADAMA BREAD
(2 LOAVES)

A New England farmer, so the legend goes, cursed with a lazy
wife who hated to cook and whose taste in breads was as low as
her energy level, decided to bake some good, rich bread for him-
self. Anna was her name, and the farmer's bread derived its
name from his feelings about her shortcomings in the baking
department.

> ½ cup white stone-ground cornmeal
> 2 cups boiling water
> 3 tablespoons butter
> ½ cup dark molasses
> 1 rounded teaspoon salt
> 1 yeast cake dissolved in ½ cup warm water
> 4 cups flour

Stir the cornmeal very slowly into the boiling water, using a

wooden spoon. When thoroughly mixed, add the butter, molasses, and salt. If there are any lumps in the mixture, rub the
whole through a sieve. Cool to lukewarm. Add the yeast dissolved in the warm water. Add the flour, 1 cup at a time, stirring
with the wooden spoon, to make a smooth dough. Place on a
lightly floured board or canvas, and knead well. Place in a large
well-buttered bowl, and cover with a cloth wrung out in hot
water. Allow to rise in a warm place, free from drafts, until
more than double its original bulk, or for about 2½ hours.

In the meantime preheat the oven to hot (375°–400°). Butter two 9-inch bread pans. Turn the dough out onto a lightly
floured board again, knead lightly, and shape into two loaves.
Place in the buttered pans, cover with waxed paper and a towel
wrung out in hot water, and allow to rise again until more than
doubled, or for about 1 hour. Place the loaves in the preheated
oven and bake until they are a deep golden brown, or for about
45 to 50 minutes. Turn out onto a cake rack to cool.

APPLESAUCE-NUT BREAD
(1 LOAF)

Preheat oven to 350°

> 2 *cups flour*
> ¾ *cup granulated sugar*
> 3 *teaspoons baking powder*
> ½ *teaspoon baking soda*
> ½ *teaspoon cinnamon*
> 1 *teaspoon salt*
> 1 *egg*
> 1 *cup applesauce*
> 3 *tablespoons melted butter*
> 1 *cup coarsely chopped walnuts*

Butter a 9-inch bread pan. Sift together once the flour, sugar, baking powder, baking soda, cinnamon, and salt and return to the sifter. Beat the egg in a medium-sized mixing bowl. Stir in the applesauce and melted butter. Sift in the dry ingredients, add the nuts, and stir with a large spoon just until blended. Place the mixture in the buttered pan, spreading it evenly. Bake about 1 hour in the preheated oven, or until the loaf tests done in the center. Allow to cool 10 minutes before turning out onto a cake rack. Do not cut until cold. Slice and serve with whipped butter.

WHOLE-WHEAT-RAISIN MUFFINS
(8 MUFFINS)

Preheat oven to 425°

 ¼ *cup raisins*
 ¾ *cup whole-wheat flour*
 ¼ *cup white flour*
 2 *teaspoons baking powder*
 ¼ *teaspoon salt*
 1 *heaping tablespoon light-brown sugar*
 1 *egg*
 ½ *cup milk*
 2 *tablespoons melted butter*

Cover the raisins with boiling water, then dry on paper toweling. Butter the muffin tins. Sift together both flours, with the baking powder, salt, and sugar. Beat the egg well, and add the milk. Add the dry ingredients and mix quickly with a spoon. Stir in the butter and raisins, and divide equally into the muffin tins. In the preheated oven, bake until lightly browned or for about 25 minutes. Serve immediately.

INDIAN PUFFS
(8 PUFFS)
Preheat oven to 425°–450°

    1 pint whole milk
    4 tablespoons white cornmeal
    1 tablespoon granulated sugar
    ¾ teaspoon salt
    3 eggs, well beaten

Butter well 8 one-cup custard cups. Scald the milk in the top part of an enamel double boiler. Place the cornmeal in a bowl and gradually stir in the scalding-hot milk. Mix until smooth and free from lumps. Add the sugar and salt. Place the mixture in the top part of the same double boiler over boiling water and cook 5 minutes, stirring constantly. Cool until lukewarm, at which time gradually add the well-beaten eggs. Fill the custard cups half full. Place them in an oblong shallow cake tin, and bake in the preheated oven until they are well puffed and brown on top, or for about 25 minutes.

Serve at once, with plenty of soft butter. If not eaten at once, they will fall like a soufflé, but in this case run a knife around the edges and turn them out onto a cake pan and they may be reheated in a 450° oven and eaten with butter and jam for breakfast, like muffins.

VERMONT JOHNNYCAKE MUFFINS
(8 MUFFINS)
Preheat oven to 400°

    1 cup sifted all-purpose flour
    2¼ teaspoons baking powder

¼ *teaspoon salt*

½ *cup cornmeal*

2 *eggs, well beaten*

⅓ *cup milk*

¼ *cup maple syrup*

6 *tablespoons melted butter*

Sift the first 3 ingredients together, add the cornmeal and sift again. Combine the remaining ingredients and add to the dry ingredients, stirring only enough to dampen all the flour. Pour into well-buttered muffin tins and bake in a hot oven for about 30 minutes, or until brown.

These are particularly delicious served with Maple Cream or Maple Butter, products that can be found in New England specialty shops.

BUTTERMILK CORNBREAD
(9 SERVINGS)

Preheat oven to 425°

1 *cup flour*

3 *teaspoons baking powder*

¼ *teaspoon baking soda*

1 *teaspoon salt*

1 *tablespoon granulated sugar*

1 *cup Rhode Island white cornmeal*

1 *egg, well beaten*

1½ *cups buttermilk*

4 *tablespoons melted butter*

Sift together the first 5 ingredients; add the cornmeal, beaten egg, and buttermilk and beat with a spoon to make a stiff, smooth batter. Stir in the melted butter, and when well mixed, pour into a well-buttered baking pan. Bake in the preheated oven until the cornbread is lightly browned on top, or for about 30 to 40 minutes. Cut into 9 squares and serve piping hot with soft butter.

CRANBERRY-ORANGE-NUT BREAD
(1 LOAF)

Preheat oven to 350°
    2 cups sifted flour
    1½ teaspoons baking powder
    1 teaspoon salt
    ½ teaspoon baking soda
    1 egg, well beaten
    Juice of 1 orange (⅓ cup)
    Grated rind of 1 orange (about 1 heaping teaspoon)
    ¼ cup cold water
    1 cup granulated sugar
    ¼ cup melted butter
    1 cup cranberries washed and cut in half
    ½ cup coarsely chopped walnuts or pecans

Butter a 9-inch bread pan. Sift the flour, measure, resift with baking powder, salt, and soda. Combine the beaten egg with the orange juice, grated rind, water, and sugar. Add the sifted ingredients and stir just long enough to mix. Stir in the melted butter. Fold in the cranberries and nuts. Place in the pan, making the corners and sides slightly higher than the center. Bake in the preheated oven for about 1 hour, or until the bread tests done in the center. Turn out on a cake rack to cool.

BOSTON BROWN BREAD
(1 LOAF)

½ cup rye meal or white flour
½ cup white cornmeal
1 cup whole-wheat flour
½ teaspoon baking powder
½ teaspoon salt
½ teaspoon baking soda
1 tablespoon boiling water
1½ cups buttermilk
½ cup light molasses
1 egg, well beaten
1 teaspoon butter
½ cup seedless raisins (optional)

Butter well a 1-quart melon mold, including the cover. Sift the first 5 ingredients together. Dissolve the soda in the boiling water. Add the water and the buttermilk to the molasses. Stir well. Add the sifted ingredients to the buttermilk-molasses mixture, stirring well until free from lumps. Add the egg to the batter, and the raisins, if desired, and mix well.

Pour the batter into the mold, cover, and place on a rack in a large covered pan containing about 2 quarts boiling water, or enough to reach the level of the bottom of the mold lid. Steam 4 hours, replacing the boiling water as it evaporates.

When cool enough to handle, lift the mold from the water, remove the cover, and turn the bread out onto a shallow pan. Bake in a preheated 400° oven for about 10 minutes to dry the bread out a bit. Slice and serve while still warm.

To reheat, wrap in foil and place in a moderate oven. Or

place in a colander over boiling water and steam for 5 to 10 minutes. Good with butter and rich hot milk and sprinkled with
salt, for breakfast instead of cereal.

PARKER HOUSE ROLLS
(3 DOZEN)

Preheat oven to 375°

      2 *cups milk, scalded*
      2 *tablespoons butter*
      2 *tablespoons granulated sugar*
      1 *level teaspoon salt*
      1 *yeast cake or envelope of dried yeast*
      ¼ *cup lukewarm water*
      5½ *to 6 cups all-purpose flour*
      4 *tablespoons soft butter*
      4 *tablespoons melted butter*

Scald the milk and stir in the butter, sugar, and salt. Place in a
large mixing bowl and cool. Dissolve the yeast in the lukewarm
water, and when well mixed, add to the cooled mixture. With
a large wooden spoon or paddle, stir in 3 cups of the flour. Mix
well until smooth and free from lumps. Cover with a cloth and
set aside to rise for about 1½ hours. Beat down with a spoon or
paddle and add gradually about 2½ cups more flour, or enough
to make a not too stiff dough. Transfer to a well-buttered large
mixing bowl. Cover with a cloth, and allow to rise again in a
warm but not too hot spot, until well doubled in bulk, or for
about 1 hour.

Turn the dough out on a well-floured pastry board or cloth
and roll out to ½-inch thickness with a rolling pin covered with
a well-floured white sock sold for the purpose. Using a 2¾-inch

round cutter, cut out as many rounds as possible. Gather up the scraps surrounding the rounds and set aside. Using the thin wooden handle of a rubber bowl-scraper, crease the center of each round. Place a small lump of soft butter on each toward the edge, fold over, and pinch together. Transfer to a well-buttered cookie sheet. Gather up the scraps into a ball, and roll out, cut, and shape as before, and place on a second buttered sheet. Cover with the cloth and allow to rise again in a warm spot, for about 1 hour longer. Brush each one lightly with melted butter and bake in a preheated oven until the rolls are a light golden brown all over, or for about 25 to 30 minutes. Serve as soon as possible with plenty of soft whipped butter, or reheat in a hot oven for a few minutes if necessary.

SPIDER CORNBREAD
(SERVES 6)

Preheat oven to 350°

1⅓ cups white cornmeal
⅓ cup all-purpose flour
1 teaspoon baking soda
½ teaspoon salt
¼ cup granulated sugar
1 cup buttermilk
2 eggs, well beaten
2 cups sweet milk
2 tablespoons butter

Mix and sift together the cornmeal, flour, soda, salt, and sugar. Add the buttermilk, eggs, and 1 cup of the sweet milk. Beat with a spoon until free from lumps. Melt the butter in a heavy 9-inch iron frying pan, and when the pan is very hot, pour in the batter. Pour over the batter the second cup of milk. Bake in the preheated oven for about 50 minutes, or until the cornbread is brown on top. Cut in pie-shaped pieces and serve at once.

SHREDDED-WHEAT BREAD
(2 LOAVES)

2 cups boiling water
2 shredded-wheat biscuits
2 teaspoons salt
⅓ cup granulated sugar
⅓ cup molasses
3 tablespoons butter
2 packages dry yeast
½ cup lukewarm water
7–8 cups all-purpose flour

Pour boiling water over the shredded wheat in a large mixing bowl. Add the salt, sugar, molasses, and butter. Stir well. Cool to lukewarm. Dissolve the yeast in the ½ cup warm water and add to the contents of the bowl. Stir well with a large spoon, adding gradually about 6 to 7 cups flour, making a very stiff dough. Cover with waxed paper and a cloth wrung out in hot water, and allow to rise in a warm spot until doubled in bulk, or for about 1 hour.

Toss out onto a well-floured pastry cloth or board and knead well, adding the rest of the flour. Divide equally and place in 2 well-buttered 9-inch bread pans. Cover again with waxed paper and a cloth wrung out in hot water. Allow to rise again until doubled in bulk, or for about 1 hour longer. Preheat the oven to 375°. When the dough has doubled in bulk, place in the oven and bake until the loaves are brown and they test done in the center, or for about 50 minutes. Turn out on a rack to cool.

SUGARY APPLE MUFFINS
(ABOUT 16 MUFFINS)

Preheat oven to 450°

>2 *small apples (1 cup when cut up)*
>2½ *cups flour*
>3½ *teaspoons baking powder*
>½ *teaspoon salt*
>½ *teaspoon grated nutmeg*
>½ *teaspoon powdered cinnamon*
>4 *tablespoons butter*
>½ *cup granulated sugar plus 2 tablespoons*
>1 *egg, well beaten*
>1 *cup milk*

First wash, peel, quarter, and core the apples. Chop into small pieces. Sift together the flour, baking powder, salt, and ¼ teaspoon each of the nutmeg and cinnamon. Cream the butter and ½ cup granulated sugar; stir in the well-beaten egg. Add the dry ingredients alternately with the milk. Fold in the prepared apples. Fill the well-buttered muffin tins almost full. Sprinkle with the additional sugar seasoned with the remainder of the cinnamon and nutmeg. Bake in the preheated oven for about 20 minutes or until the muffins test done. Eat while hot, with plenty of whipped sweet or salty butter.

BLUEBERRY MUFFINS
(ABOUT 15 LARGE MUFFINS)

Preheat oven to 350°–375°

>2 *cups flour*
>½ *cup granulated sugar*
>2½ *teaspoons baking powder*

½ teaspoon salt
½ teaspoon cinnamon
¼ teaspoon nutmeg
1 egg
¾ cup milk
¼ cup melted butter
¼ cup washed and floured blueberries

Sift together into a bowl the flour, sugar, baking powder, salt, cinnamon, and nutmeg. Beat together the egg and milk. Gradually add to the flour mixture, making a stiff but well-mixed dough. Stir in the melted butter and fold in the blueberries. Place in well-buttered muffin tins and bake in the preheated oven until the muffins are lightly browned on top, or for about 25 minutes.

HOT CROSS BUNS
(2 DOZEN)

4 cups sifted flour
½ teaspoon salt
¾ to 1 teaspoon cinnamon
1 cup currants and seedless raisins mixed
1 cup milk
¼ cup butter
⅓ cup granulated sugar
¾ teaspoon powdered yeast
¼ cup lukewarm water
1 egg, well beaten

Sift the flour, salt, and cinnamon into a large bowl. Wash the currants and raisins and dry well. Add these to the flour and stir. Scald the milk with the butter and sugar, and cool to lukewarm. Soften the yeast in the water and add it to the cooled milk. Beat the egg well and stir into the milk and yeast. Pour into a hollow made in the dry ingredients, mix to a dough, and knead as you would bread, on a lightly floured board or canvas. Place in a well-buttered bowl, cover with waxed paper and a cloth wrung out in hot water, and allow to rise in a warm place, free from drafts, until very light and at least double its original size. This should take about 2 hours.

Divide into equal portions as for rolls, shaping them lightly into 24 equal-sized balls. Place on two well-greased cookie sheets, a little distance apart. Let rise again until very light, or for about 1½ hours. Mark a cross on top of each with the blade of a knife dipped in flour.

Preheat the oven to 400°. Bake the buns for about 15 to 20 minutes. When they are almost done, brush over with milk, sprinkle lightly with superfine sugar, and return to the oven for about 1 minute. Remove the pans from the oven and cool partially. In the meantime make the following icing to be used for the sugar cross on each bun.

ICING

>2 *cups or more confectioner's sugar*
>*About 3 tablespoons hot milk*
>1 *teaspoon butter*
>1 *teaspoon vanilla*
>½ *teaspoon almond extract*

Sift 2 cups confectioner's sugar into a bowl. Heat together the milk and butter, and stir gradually into the sugar. The mixture should be thick enough to hold together when squeezed from a pastry bag. If necessary add more confectioner's sugar. Flavor with the vanilla and almond extract. Place the mixture in a pastry bag with a suitable tip and make a neat cross on each bun.

ELEVEN

Griddle Cakes & Their Relatives

RHODE ISLAND GRIDDLE CAKES
(SERVES 2–4)

Sift together 2 cups water-ground johnnycake cornmeal with 1 cup flour, 1 teaspoon salt, a big pinch of powdered ginger. Gradually stir in enough sour milk to make a stiff batter. Dissolve 1 tablespoon molasses in a little warm water, add 1 teaspoon soda and stir until it foams up. Then stir into the batter and bake on a hot griddle like pancakes. Serve with them a bowl of butter creamed with powdered sugar, flavored with powdered cinnamon.

VERMONT WHOLE-WHEAT POT-CHEESE
GRIDDLE CAKES
(SERVES 4)

½ cup whole-wheat flour
½ teaspoon baking powder
½ teaspoon salt
1 teaspoon sugar
1 cup pot cheese
¾ cup light cream or milk
1 egg, well beaten

Sift together the flour, baking powder, salt, and sugar. Moisten the pot cheese with the cream or milk. Beat the egg and stir in the creamed pot cheese. Sift in the dry ingredients and mix well. Bake on a lightly buttered griddle (preferably Teflon), using a heaping tablespoonful for each cake. Turn over with a pancake turner when well browned on the first side. When well done on the second side, serve on hot plates with butter and maple syrup, or top with sour cream or yogurt and sprinkle with grated maple sugar.

VERMONT HUMPTY DOES
(SERVES 1)

1 egg
½ cup pot-style cottage cheese
2 tablespoons sour cream
Scant ¼ teaspoon salt
2 tablespoons all-purpose flour

Beat the egg, add the cheese, sour cream, and salt. Mix well with a spoon. Add the flour and stir until smooth. Heat the griddle (preferably Teflon), butter lightly, and drop the mixture with a tablespoon onto the greased griddle, making 6 cakes. When brown on the underside, turn and cook until brown on the second side. Serve at once on a hot plate. Spread with whipped butter and maple syrup and purr contentedly while eating them.

CORN PUFFS
(SERVES 6—ABOUT 2 PUFFS PER PERSON)

2 *cups cooked fresh or one 12-ounce can whole-kernel corn*
½ *teaspoon salt*
3 *tablespoons milk*
2 *tablespoons all-purpose flour*
2 *large eggs, separated*
2 *or 3 tablespoons vegetable oil, for frying*

Mix the first 4 ingredients together, using a large fork. Beat the egg whites until stiff, then, using the same beater, beat the yolks. Stir the yolks into the corn mixture, then fold in the whites gently. Have ready a large, heavy frying pan. Add the oil, and heat until almost smoking hot. Drop the mixture by large table-spoonfuls into the hot fat, and cook until the puffs are brown on one side (about 1 minute), turn over with a pancake turner and brown the second side. Place on a hot platter and serve at once, with butter and/or maple syrup.

MAPLE-SUGAR TOAST
(SERVES 4–8)

This may be made with any white or sweet bread, but is particularly good made with Lithuanian Bread (page 160).

Preheat the broiling unit

    8 slices bread, cut ½ inch thick
    ¼ pound (1 bar) butter at room temperature
    6–8 tablespoons maple sugar

Spread the 8 slices of bread out on a large flat cookie sheet. Toast one side under the broiler, turn the slices over, and butter copiously while hot. Sprinkle the sugar over all. Place under the broiler and watch carefully until the sugar melts and is sizzling hot. Serve at once.

THIN EAST-OF-NARRAGANSETT JOHNNYCAKES
(SERVES 4)

Preheat oven to 475°

    1 cup fresh white stone-ground cornmeal
    ¾ teaspoon salt
    1 cup boiling water
    ¾ cup cold milk (about)
    1 strip bacon wrapped around a fork

Have ready a cookie sheet on which to place the johnnycakes as you make them. Place the cornmeal in an oven-proof bowl and stir in the salt. Place the bowl in a hot oven to heat the cornmeal. Stir once or twice. Remove from the oven and stir in gradually the boiling water, mixing it well, making a thick paste, as free from lumps as possible. Then stir in the cold milk gradually.

In the meantime heat a large, heavy iron frying pan or griddle, rubbing it with the bacon. When the meal is well softened and smooth, drop a tablespoon of the mixture onto the lightly greased but very hot frying pan. The meal should spread to about ⅛-inch thickness, and should be about the size of a small pancake. If it doesn't spread thin enough, cautiously add a very little more milk to the batter. Remove the trial cake and discard it. Rub the frying pan again with the bacon, and make 8 cakes of equal size. Cook over reasonably hot heat until they are a golden brown on one side, or for about 5 minutes, then turn over with a pancake turner and cook until brown on the other side, or for about 5 minutes longer. Place immediately on the cookie sheet and place in the hot oven while you start the second batch, rubbing the pan again with the bacon. Serve the cooked and slightly puffed hot cakes on hot plates to your guests or family, to be spread lavishly with butter and maple syrup or sugar. In the meantime find time to turn the second batch of cakes and brown the other side. Then place in the oven as before to puff and crisp a bit—ready for second helpings.

THICK WEST-OF-NARRAGANSETT JOHNNYCAKES
(SERVES 4–6)

Preheat oven to 450°

    2 cups fresh Rhode Island stone-ground white cornmeal
    1 scant teaspoon salt
    About 3½ cups boiling water
    About ½ cup milk
    Beef drippings or bacon fat, for frying

Put the cornmeal into a large oven-proof bowl and place in the preheated oven to heat through thoroughly, but not long enough to scorch it. Remove the bowl from the oven, holding the bowl with a pot holder, and stir in the salt, then moisten gradually with the boiling water, using just enough to make a very stiff paste. Then gradually add just sufficient milk to smooth the whole. The mixture should be smooth and free from lumps, but not at all liquid. It should be just thick enough to be dropped by heaping tablespoonfuls, making oval-shaped cakes about 3½ inches long, 2 inches wide, and ½ inch thick.

Drop onto a hot, well-greased iron griddle or frying pan of generous proportions, making 12 cakes in all. Do not squash them down. Cook slowly 15 minutes on one side before turning over. At this point you may press lightly on each with the pancake turner, so that they will be smooth on the other side. Cook 15 minutes longer, adding a very little additional fat to the griddle if necessary. When they are done, place them on a large cookie sheet and place in the hot oven to puff them up a bit. Serve with crisp bacon or sausages, accompanied by plenty of butter and maple syrup, or, better still, Maple Cream or Maple Butter (see page 198).

HASTY PUDDING
(SERVES 6)

Hasty pudding is traditionally served on Ash Wednesday.

> *1 cup yellow or white cornmeal*
> *1 cup cold water*
> *3 cups boiling water*
> *1 teaspoon salt*

Mix the dry cornmeal into the cold water. Heat 3 cups of water in the top part of a large double boiler, and when it comes to a boil, add the salt, and gradually stir in the moistened cornmeal. Cook on low heat, stirring constantly with a wooden spoon, until well thickened, smooth, and free from lumps. Then place over boiling water, cover, and continue cooking, stirring occasionally, until the mixture is very thick, or for about 1 hour. Serve hot, with molasses or sugar and butter or rich milk.

FRIED CORNMEAL MUSH
(SERVES 6)

Cook exactly as you would Hasty Pudding (above), adding, however, 4 tablespoons flour to the dry cornmeal before mixing it with the cold water. This makes it easier to slice. When done, pack into straight-sided drinking glasses which have been rinsed in cold water. When ready to use, unmold and cut into even ½-inch thick slices, flour lightly on both sides, and fry slowly on a lightly greased skillet until golden brown, turning the slices over to brown both sides. Serve on hot plates with plenty of butter and maple syrup or honey.

VERMONT OATCAKES
(MAKES 18 CAKES)

Preheat oven to 325°–350°

> 2 *cups stone-ground oat flour*
> ½ *cup (1 bar) soft butter and more*
> ⅓ *cup all-purpose cream*
> 4 *tablespoons pure maple syrup*
> Scant ½ *teaspoon salt*

Butter copiously 2 shallow 8-inch square cake pans. Sift the oat flour into a bowl. Add the ½ cup butter and mix it in well, using a wire pastry blender. Mix the cream, maple syrup, and salt together, and add gradually to the flour and butter. When well mixed, butter your fingertips, place half of the mixture in each pan, and with the aid of a large fork and your fingertips press out the mixture, so as to cover the bottom of each pan evenly with the dough. With the dull side of a knife mark the surface of each lightly so as to make 9 equal squares in each pan. Dot each square with a small bit of butter, and bake for about 25 minutes or until firm and lightly browned. Cool completely before cutting through the dough to separate the squares. With the aid of a small spatula remove the squares carefully and place on a flat cookie sheet. Dot again with a small quantity of butter and reheat before serving. Good with soup, or with jam for tea.

MRS. CAHILL'S PLUM PORRIDGE
(SERVES 4–6)
1 *cup seedless raisins*
⅔ *cup water*
½ *cup granulated sugar*
1 *quart whole milk*
2 *generous tablespoons all-purpose flour*
2 *eggs*
Pinch *of salt*
1 *scant teaspoon powdered cinnamon*

Wash the raisins, cover with the ⅔ cup water, add ¼ cup of the sugar and boil gently until the raisins are plump, or for about 10 to 15 minutes. Set aside.

Heat the milk in the top part of a double boiler over boiling water. Mix together the flour and the remaining ¼ cup sugar. Beat the eggs slightly, add the sugar and flour and beat until smooth. Add a little of the hot milk and mix well, then add gradually to the hot milk, stirring constantly over boiling water until the mixture coats the spoon, or for about 8 to 10 minutes. Remove from the heat entirely and add the raisins, a pinch of salt, and the powdered cinnamon. Serve while still hot in porridge bowls. Serve oyster crackers or puffed Boston Common Crackers (page 4) with this.

CORN DODGERS
(1 DOZEN)

Preheat oven to 450°

 1½ *cups white cornmeal*
 1 *teaspoon salt*
 ¼ *pound butter*
 1¼ *cups water*

Put the cornmeal and salt in a bowl. Bring the butter and the water to a boil. Stir this into the cornmeal until you have a thick mush. Drop by tablespoonfuls onto a well-buttered cookie sheet. Bake about 20 minutes or until brown on the bottom and lightly brown on top. Serve at once.

TWELVE

Jellies, Jams, Preserves, &
Wines

GENERAL DIRECTIONS FOR MAKING JELLY

For jelly-making, select fruit that is firm and in good condition, on the underripe rather than overripe side (though a certain proportion of thoroughly ripe fruit adds greatly to the flavor).

The first process is to extract the juice. Pick over, wash in cold water, and stem all the fruit, but do not peel apples. Crush berries, currants, grapes, and soft fruits to start the juice flowing, and add a little water. Apples and quinces require water to cover. Cook soft fruits 10 minutes or until soft. Cook hard fruits about 25 minutes. When the fruit is soft, turn into a jelly bag or into a colander lined with several thicknesses of cheesecloth wrung out in hot water. Allow the juice to drain into a deep pan. Do not squeeze, but shift the fruit occasionally. (The remaining pulp may have water added to cover and be recooked to make a separate second extraction of second-quality jelly. Keep this extraction separate from the first, however.)

Measure the juice, then boil 5 minutes, skimming it carefully during the process. When the juice has cooked 5 minutes, add the required amount of sugar (usually equal to the juice, although some fruits require less). Then cook the juice and sugar together until the mixture is ready to jell. Use a deep kettle, of a capacity 4 or 5 times as great as the amount of juice to be cooked, as jelly has a great tendency to boil up and over. The time required for this second cooking varies, but the quicker, the better, is the best rule.

You may use a thermometer, which at sea level should register between 218° and 221°, but the good old sheet test for doneness is the best method, in my opinion. To test, lift a spoonful of the boiling juice about a foot above the kettle and, holding the spoon so that the juice may run out the side, let the juice pour back into the kettle. If the last part of the juice forms a thin sheet as it falls off, leaving a clean edge to the spoon, the jelly is done.

Remove the jelly instantly from the fire and pour it into sterilized jars or glasses.

When the jelly has set and is cold, cover with a ¼-inch coating of hot melted paraffin. Melt the wax in a small pan, but do not heat to the smoking point. Pour a small quantity over the jelly and let it harden, then repeat, tilting the glass so that the wax covers the whole surface well.

If you have skimmed the juice frequently as it cooked, you will now have a crystal-clear jelly.

When the paraffin has hardened completely, you may add lids, though they are not essential.

Label your jars, date, and store in a cool, dark, dry place.

Note: A word of warning. Melting paraffin can be disastrous if it catches fire, as it does quite easily. To be safe, break the paraffin in small pieces and place it in a small pitcher. Put the pitcher in a saucepan of hot water and let the wax melt over a slow fire as the water is brought to a boil.

HOW TO STERILIZE GLASS JARS

Wash the jars and lids thoroughly in soapy water and rinse well. Place the jars in a large preserving kettle on a rack; fill and surround them with water. Cover the kettle and bring the water to a lively boil. (If you don't have a preserving kettle, substitute a large roasting pan, leaving a rack on the bottom.)

Scald the covers and rubbers in a separate pan.

Remove the jars, covers, and rubbers from the water with tongs, drain well, and place on a towel-covered tray.

GENERAL DIRECTIONS FOR MAKING JAM

Fruit for jam should also be free from blemishes—and again some underripe fruit is desirable. First, stem, wash, and drain it.

Some people cook the fruit before adding the sugar, but I make a syrup of sugar and water in the proportion of 1 cup water to every 5 cups sugar, boil it 5 minutes, and pour it over the fruit, then cook the mixture until it sheets from the spoon and the fruit is transparent. Proportionately less sugar is used than for jelly, or about ⅔ as much sugar as you have of prepared fruit.

Again, the quicker you cook it, the better. Skim carefully and constantly during the cooking process; also it is wise to stir the mixture frequently with a long wooden spoon.

When it is done, pour it into sterilized jars, adjust new rubber rings, and cover tightly.

BEACH-PLUM JELLY
(ABOUT 6 HALF-PINT JARS)
6 *cups beach plums*
½ *to 1 cup water*
6 *cups granulated sugar (approximately)*

Place the prepared plums in a large, sturdy saucepan and pour over them ½ cup water. Cover and cook over moderate heat for about 5 minutes. Check, and if the plums do not seem to be making their own juice sufficiently, add the remaining ½ cup water. At this point, crush the plums with a wire potato masher. Continue cooking until the plums are mushy, or for about 20 to 30 minutes, stirring when necessary. Strain through cheesecloth, allowing to drip thoroughly. Measure the juice and stir in the sugar, using a scant cup for each cup of juice. Mix thoroughly and bring rapidly to a boil, then reduce the heat to a simmer and cook uncovered for 30 to 45 minutes or until done. Seal while hot (see page 217).

PINK FOX AND CONCORD GRAPE JELLY
(4 HALF-PINT GLASSES)
8 *cups ripe Concord grapes*
5 *cups nearly ripe Pink Fox grapes*
3⅔ *cups granulated sugar*

Wash the grapes in cold water, stem, and wash again. Place in a large saucepan and crush with a potato masher. Bring to a boil and cook 10 minutes. Drain for about 2 hours; this should yield about 5½ cups of almost clear juice. Bring to a boil, skim, and stir in the sugar. Continue cooking, skimming constantly, for about 20 minutes. Pour into jars and seal when cold (see page 217).

WINEBERRY JELLY
(ABOUT 4 HALF-PINT JARS)
2 quarts (8 cups) wineberries
Granulated sugar
4 teaspoons Framboise liqueur (preferably white)

Wash the berries, place in a large enamel pan, and crush with a potato masher. Cook for a few minutes until soft, then drain twice through cheesecloth. This should give about 2 cups clear juice. Add an equal quantity of sugar. Cook until ready to jell, about 10 minutes. Add the Framboise liqueur, stir, and pour into jars. Seal when cold (see page 217).

BLUEBERRY JAM
(3 HALF-PINT JARS)
1 quart blueberries
½ cup cold water
4½ cups granulated sugar
Grated rind and juice of 1 lemon

Stem and wash the blueberries, place in a deep pan, and add the water, sugar, lemon juice and rind. Place over low heat and bring gradually to the boiling point, stirring constantly, or for about 10 minutes. Cook rapidly for 2 to 3 minutes, skimming carefully. When done, place in jars, leaving about ½ inch of space. Seal when cold (see page 217).

BLACK-CHERRY JAM
(3 HALF-PINT JARS)
2 *pounds black cherries*
2½ *cups granulated sugar*
½ *cup water*

Wash, stem, and pit the cherries. Moisten the sugar with water, bring to a boil, and boil 5 minutes, skimming if necessary. Place the cherries in a large enamel pan and pour hot syrup over them. Stir, bring to a boil, and cook, skimming and stirring as necessary, until the mixture is thick and syrupy, or for about 20 minutes. Pour into jars; seal when cold (see page 217).

CITRUS MARMALADE
(ABOUT 13 HALF-PINT GLASSES)
1 *large thin-skinned grapefruit*
2 *large navel oranges*
2 *lemons*
14 *to* 15 *cups granulated sugar*

Wash the grapefruit, oranges, and lemons. Cut each in 8 pieces and then, using a sharp knife, slice crosswise through the pulp and skin in very thin slices. Do this on a platter so as not to lose any juice. Discard the seeds and the tough part of the white membrane in the centers. Measure and place in a large enamel pan. Cover with twice the measure of cold water. (This amount of fruit should make about 7 cups fruit, so you should cover it with about 14 cups water.) Soak overnight. The next day bring gently to a boil and simmer 20 minutes. Let stand until the third day. Measure again. The fruit will have absorbed some of the water, and some will have evaporated, so the chances are you will have 14 or 15 cups. Bring gently to a boil and add an equal amount of granulated sugar. Stir well and cook until the mixture is thick and a light amber color, about 2 to 2¼ hours. Watch carefully and skim as necessary. When done, ladle into glasses. Pour a small quantity of paraffin over the hot marmalade and repeat a few hours later to seal (see page 217).

PLUMP PRESERVED STRAWBERRIES
(3 HALF-PINT JARS)
1 quart perfect ripe strawberries
3 cups granulated sugar

Wash the strawberries and remove the hulls. Place the berries in a 2-quart pan and add 1 cup sugar. Stir lightly to distribute the sugar. Place on low heat and bring to a boil, stirring lightly as the syrup forms. Skim carefully while it cooks for 5 minutes. Add a second cup of sugar, and boil another 5 minutes, skimming carefully. Add a third cup of sugar, bring to a boil, and cook 5 minutes longer. Spread this out on an oven-proof rectangular dish, and leave overnight. The next morning, ladle the cold strawberries and their juices into jars and cover tightly.

QUINCE PRESERVES
(2 PINT-SIZE JARS)
6 large quinces (about 3 pounds)
4 cups cold water
4 cups granulated sugar (2 pounds)

Wash, peel, quarter, and core 6 quinces, placing them immediately into cold water to prevent discoloration. (Be careful to remove all the white part under the cores.) Drain, cut into fairly small pieces, and place in a large enamel pan. Cover with cold water (about 4 cups). Bring slowly to a boil, and cook gently until almost soft (about ½ hour), skimming carefully. Sprinkle 1 cup of the sugar over the fruit, but do not stir. When it comes to a boil again, add the remaining 3 cups sugar (1 cup at a time), allowing the mixture to come to a boil each time, skimming without stirring. Continue cooking until it becomes a lovely red color, or for about 1¾ hours in all. Ladle into jars, and when cold, cover tightly.

PLUM CONSERVE
(3 HALF-PINT JARS)

2 *pounds ripe blue plums*
1 *cup cold water*
1 *lemon, quartered*
2½ *cups granulated sugar*
½ *cup seedless raisins, washed and drained*
¼ *cup shelled pecans, cut in two*

Remove the stems from the plums, quarter them with a sharp knife, and pull off the skins. Discard the pits, but save the skins. Place the skins in a small pan with the cold water, add the lemon, and boil together for about 5 minutes, then strain. This should give you about ¾ cup red juice. Pour this over the plums, which have been placed in a deep large pan. Stir in the sugar and the raisins. Bring to a boil and cook until thickened, or for about 30 minutes, stirring frequently and skimming as necessary. When done, add the nuts and pour into the sterilized jars, and seal tightly.

MARGARET'S SOUTHWEST HARBOR, MAINE, RHUBARB-AND-PINEAPPLE CONSERVE
(ABOUT 4 CUPS)

1 quart fresh tender rhubarb (preferably the pink variety) (about 2 bunches)

1 cup canned crushed pineapple

4 cups granulated sugar

Strained juice of 1 navel orange

Grated rind of 1 navel orange

¼ cup coarsely cut pecan meats

Remove the leaves and about 1 inch of the root end of the rhubarb. Wash the rhubarb thoroughly and cut in 1-inch pieces. Do not peel. Place in a large enamel saucepan and add the pineapple, sugar, orange juice, and grated rind. Bring to a boil, then cook slowly until thick, stirring occasionally. Skim once or twice. This will take about 30 minutes. Add the pecans about 5 minutes before the conserve is done. Pour into sterilized jars and cover while hot.

CONCORD GRAPE CONSERVE
(ABOUT 7 PINTS)

6 pounds Concord grapes

2 navel oranges

7 cups granulated sugar

1 teaspoon salt

1½ cups seeded or seedless raisins

3 ounces (about ¾ cup) broken pecans

First wash the grapes in cold water. Stem them and wash once more in running cold water. Now proceed with the tedious job of slipping the skins from the grapes, keeping them separate from the pulp. Quarter the oranges, and with a sharp knife cut away the white center parts, removing any seeds there may be. Squeeze each section with your fingers to extract most of the juice, which must be kept carefully. Now put the sections, peel and all, through a meat grinder, using the medium cutter. Add this to the orange juice. Boil the grape pulp in a large pan for about 10 minutes, counting from the time it comes to a boil. Skim carefully and stir constantly with a wooden spoon to prevent sticking. Strain through a fine sieve placed over a large pan, pressing well with a spoon to extract all the pulp. Discard the seeds and add the sugar and salt to the pulp. Stir until the sugar has dissolved; add the orange rind, pulp, and juice, and the raisins. Boil rapidly, stirring constantly, for about 10 to 15 minutes, or until the mixture begins to thicken. Skim carefully. At this point add the skins and boil 10 to 15 minutes longer, stirring constantly and skimming frequently. Remove from fire, add the pecans, stir well, and pour immediately into sterilized jars. Cover when cold.

MRS. COOLIDGE'S TOMATO CONSERVE
(7 HALF-PINT JARS)

4 pounds ripe tomatoes
1½ oranges
1 lemon
12 whole cloves
3 1-inch-long sticks of cinnamon bark
*Granulated sugar equal in weight to the combined fruits when
  prepared for cooking*

*⅓ cup thinly sliced candied or, better still, preserved-in-syrup
  ginger (optional)*

Plunge the tomatoes one by one into boiling water and then into
cold to facilitate the removal of skins. Slice fine and set aside.
Wash and quarter the oranges, halve the lemon and slice very
thin, discarding the seeds. Pour off excess juice from the tomatoes, add the oranges and lemon, and weigh. Measure out an
equal weight of granulated sugar. Place the tomatoes, fruit, sugar,
cloves, and cinnamon in a large shallow kettle and bring quickly
to a boil, stirring frequently with a wooden spoon. Reduce the
heat somewhat, skim as necessary, and boil until thickened,
about 1 hour. Watch carefully, as the mixture scorches easily.
Ten minutes before it is done, add the candied or preserved
ginger, if you like ginger. (I do. Mrs. Coolidge doesn't.) When
done, pour into sterilized jars. Cover tightly.

CRANBERRY-DATE RELISH
(5–6 half-pint jars)

4 cups raw cranberries
1 cup sugar
1 cup dates, pitted and cut in small pieces
½ cup seedless raisins
2 cups water
¼ cup cider vinegar
¼ teaspoon cinnamon
¼ teaspoon ginger

Stem and wash the cranberries and combine with the sugar,
dates, raisins, water, vinegar, and spices in a large saucepan.
Bring to a boil. Skim carefully and cook rapidly for about 10

minutes, stirring occasionally to prevent scorching. Pour into sterilized jars, and when cold, cover tightly.

CRANBERRY SAUCE DE LUXE
(4 HALF-PINT JARS)
4 *dozen blanched almonds*
1 *pound fresh cranberries*
2 *cups granulated sugar*
1 *cup cold water*
6 *generous tablespoons Citrus Marmalade* (*page 221*)
Strained juice of 2 lemons

Blanch 4 dozen almonds by pouring boiling water over them. Let them stand 2 or 3 minutes, then pour off the water, and the brown skins should pinch off easily. Cover the almonds with cold water and set aside.

Wash and pick over the cranberries, discarding any imperfect ones and any stems encountered. Moisten the sugar with the cold water, stir, bring to a boil, skim carefully, and boil 5 minutes. Then add the cranberries and cook 3 to 5 minutes longer, or until they have all popped open and become transparent. Remove from the fire and add the Citrus Marmalade; stir, and when melted, add the lemon juice. Add the well-drained blanched almonds, pour into sterilized jars, and cover. Serve well chilled with roast chicken, turkey or pheasant.

ROSE-HIP SYRUP
(ABOUT 3 CUPS)
2 *pounds rose hips* (*ripe and red*)
Water to cover
1 *pound 2 ounces granulated sugar*

Wash the hips thoroughly and put into a large aluminum sauce-pan. Cover well with cold water (measure the amount neces-sary). Bring to a boil. Simmer about 10 minutes, or until tender. Mash well with a wooden masher. Put into a jelly bag and squeeze out as much juice as possible. Return the pulp to the pan and add as much cold water as before. Bring to a boil and simmer 5 to 10 minutes. Put back into the jelly bag and squeeze again. Discard the pulp. Mix the two lots of juice and pour into a clean jelly bag. Allow to drip into a clean pan overnight. Boil the juice down until only 3 cups of it remain. Add the sugar. Stir until dissolved. Boil for 5 minutes, skimming if necessary. Pour into sterilized bottles at once and seal or cork.

DELAWARE OR TOKAY GREEN-GRAPE JUICE
(COOKED VARIETY)
(2 QUARTS)

An unusual, delicate-flavored beverage.

> 12 *cups ripe green grapes, picked from stems*
> 1 *quart water*
> 2 *cups granulated sugar*

Wash the grapes, stem them, wash again. Place in a large deep pan, and add the water. Bring slowly to a boil and simmer 15 minutes. Strain through a sieve into another pan. Discard seeds. Strain twice through a jelly bag or cheesecloth, allowing the juice to run or drip through without squeezing. Bring the juice to a boil and skim carefully. Set aside for a minute or two and then bring to a second boil. Skim and stir in the sugar. Bring to a boil and boil for one minute. Pour into hot sterilized jars on which you have already placed the sterilized rubbers, filling them to the brim. Add a little boiling water if necessary. Cover with sterilized lids and seal tight (see page 217).

CONCORD GRAPE JUICE (UNCOOKED VARIETY)
(6 QUARTS)

12 cups Concord grapes, picked from stems
6 cups granulated sugar
About 3 quarts boiling water

Wash the grapes in cold water, stem them, wash once more, and drain well. Put 2 cups of the grapes in each sterilized jar and add to each a cup of sugar. Fill the jars to overflowing with boiling water, cover, and seal tight. Shake the jars until the sugar has dissolved. Let stand 2 to 3 weeks before using. When ready to use, strain the contents of the jars, discarding the grapes. By then the juice should be a lively clear red, instead of the purple of commercial grape juice.

MRS. CORDEIRO'S BEET WINE
(6 QUARTS)

5 large beets
6 quarts cold water and more
4 pounds granulated sugar
2 packages (15 ounces) seedless black raisins
2 yeast cakes

Scrub the beets, remove the stems, and cut them in pieces, leaving the skins on. In a kettle, cover with the cold water. Put them to boil for 2 hours, then strain, discarding the beets but saving the juice. Add enough more water to make 6 quarts of liquid.

When lukewarm, add the sugar, stir well, and add the raisins and yeast cakes. Stir every day for ten days. Strain through cheesecloth, and allow to stand 1 day and 1 night. Then put into sterilized jars, but do not seal tightly.

MRS. CORDEIRO'S WILD-CHERRY WINE
(5 QUARTS)

2 *quarts ripe wild cherries, stems removed*
Cold water to cover
4 *pounds granulated sugar*
Another quart of water, later

Wash the cherries, place in a deep earthenware crock, and mash well with a potato masher. Cover with cold water and allow to stand two days. Place large strainer over a pot and drain, saving the juice and discarding the cherries. Add the sugar to the juice and another quart of water, put back into the crock, and let ferment until it has stopped working, probably from 2 to 3 months. (Mrs. Cordeiro says the longer it ferments, the better.) When the wine is ready, pour it into clean bottles. Cover the bottles, but do not cork tightly for three or four days. (The wine may burst the bottles if they are tightly corked too soon.)

ELDERBERRY-FLOWER WINE
(ABOUT 3½ QUARTS)

1 *quart freshly picked elderberry blossoms*
1 *gallon boiling water*
3 *pounds (6 cups) granulated sugar*
1 *cake yeast*

1 *cup lukewarm water*
½ *pound chopped seeded raisins*

Strip the tiny white flowers from the elderberry blossoms until you have 1 quart of them. Discard the stems. Boil together for 5 minutes the gallon of water and the sugar. Dissolve the yeast in the lukewarm water. Pour the boiling hot syrup over the elderberry blossoms and allow to cool a while (about ½ hour), then stir in the yeast water. Place in a large crock, cover, and allow the mixture to stand 3 days, then strain out the blossoms through several thicknesses of clean cheesecloth, rinsed first in hot water, then in cold. Add the chopped raisins, stir, cover again, and allow to stand in a cool place until the mixture stops fermenting or working, or for about 1 month. Strain out the raisins and discard them. Strain the remaining liquid again through a fine sieve lined with four thicknesses of cheesecloth rinsed in boiling water, then in cold water. Bottle and cork the wine, label and store it in a cool place for 1 year before drinking.

DANDELION WINE
(5 QUARTS)

1 *quart dandelion blossoms*
4 *quarts boiling water*
3 *lemons*
3 *oranges*
2 *yeast cakes or envelopes of yeast*
¼ *cup lukewarm water*
8 *cups (4 pounds) granulated sugar*

Early some morning, as soon after dawn as possible, go out into the fields and gather dandelion blossoms (the flowers are still closed, which is considered to make a better wine). Do not include any of the stems. Wash them in cold water, place in a large enamel pan, and pour over them 4 quarts boiling water. Allow to soak 24 hours in a warm place. The next day, strain through cheesecloth rinsed out in hot water. Place the liquid in a large enamel pan, and add the lemons and oranges, sliced fine and seeded. Dissolve the yeast in ¼ cup warm water, and add to the rest of the ingredients along with the sugar. Stir well. Cover with waxed paper and allow to soak 3 full days and nights. Strain out the fruit. Bottle, but do not put the corks in tightly. Keep in a cool place for about 1 month. The wine will be working during this time, and tiny bubbles may be seen as it does so. At the end of the month, you will see a layer of sediment at the bottom of the bottles. This should be eliminated by pouring off the clear part and funneling into 5 clean bottles, preferably colorless ones. Cork loosely again and allow to stand about 4 weeks longer. Then cork securely and keep in a cool place.

Index